THE INVESTOR'S GUIDE TO

CONVERTIBLE BONDS

Thomas C. Noddings

DOW JONES-IRWIN
Homewood, Illinois 60430

ISBN 0-87094-288-3
Library of Congress Catalog Card No. 81-71744
Printed in the United States of America

1 2 3 4 5 6 7 8 9 0 K 9 8 7 6 5 4 3 2

PREFACE

The past 10 years have been one of the most difficult periods for investors to accumulate wealth. Individuals and institutional investors alike have witnessed a steady deterioration of the purchasing power of their assets from both high inflation and high taxes.

Is it any wonder, then, that investors, striving feverishly to keep up, are jumping from one hot new fad to another: gold, diamonds, commodities, collectibles? Alas, their chances for success are reduced every time they incur the exorbitant commissions and middleman profits as they switch among these speculations. Others succumb to tax shelter salesmen promoting nonproductive ventures solely for tax avoidance purposes. Most investors, I suspect, are weary of these pseudo investments and long for the day when they can once again put their money to work in American industry via common stocks and corporate bonds and watch their assets grow.

I don't know if the good old days will ever return. But I do know there are profitable investment strategies available today within the framework of our nation's capital markets. This is what this book is all about.

Convertible bonds offer one of the best ways to optimize total return on investment while tuning out doomsayers hawking wares that are guaranteed to increase their wealth, but not yours. Attractive investment opportunities in the area of convertible securities do exist. Familiarizing yourself with the material in this book will be time well spent.

82- 9575

Recognizing that all investors are not alike, I have structured this book with two major goals in mind. First, the material is comprehensive, but the examples are carefully designed to facilitate ease of understanding and the necessary arithmetic should not be hard to follow. My basic objective is to present a lucid discourse on convertible securities that anyone experienced with common stocks and corporate bonds can comprehend.

Next, for investors who want more advanced information and detailed support data for material covered in the text, I have provided appropriate appendixes immediately following each chapter. Students of the market should study the appendixes thoroughly; others may scan them and proceed directly to the next chapter for reading continuity.

This book is the result of years of research and actual experience and includes contributions from many investment professionals—some through direct consultation and others by their writings. I am especially indebted to Earl Zazove, of E. Zazove and Associates, a Chicago-based investment advisory firm. Dr. Zazove made invaluable contributions during the countless hours of analysis and development of the concepts and strategies you are about to learn.

Others provided much appreciated help in the actual preparation and editing of the manuscript. They include my brokerage partners Consuelo Castanuela and Carol Sachs, and Joyce Nitsche of E. Zazove and Associates. Without their help it would not have been possible for me to make this book a definitive work.

Thomas C. Noddings

CONTENTS

v

4. **Hedging convertible bonds with common stock** 141

The Energy Resources 9s of 1995 convertible bond: *Risk-reward analysis. Convertible hedge positions in Energy Resources.* Managing a convertible bond hedge portfolio: *Research. Risk-reward analysis. Selecting the best hedge posture. Establishing hedge positions. Monitoring the hedge portfolio. Trading the short side. Closing out hedge positions.* Actual hedging experience. Hedging on margin.

5. **Hedging convertibles with put and call options** 177

When not to use puts and calls. When to use puts and calls. Hedging the LTV Corporation 12s of 2005 convertible bond. Convertible/option hedges in Zenith Radio: *Call option hedges. Which call to sell. Put option hedges. Put and call option hedges combined.* Managing a convertible/option hedge portfolio. Actual investment experience.

6. **The convertible strategies line** 219

Designing your portfolio. Actual investment experience. A final word from the author.

INTRODUCTION

This book is about convertible securities—convertible bonds and convertible preferred stocks. Ignored by the investment community in the past, this special area of the market is in a period of rapid expansion. I know from years of experience that an understanding of convertibles can be the most profitable knowledge an investor can acquire. Compared to conventional instruments like common stocks or corporate bonds, a portfolio of carefully managed convertibles can provide greater capital appreciation, less risk, higher income, or any combination of these important benefits.

In this book we will explore the unique world of convertibles, beginning with basic selection procedures and concluding with aggressive portfolio management. I will also present advanced hedging strategies currently being employed by the most sophisticated investors. But before we begin the journey into the world of convertible investing, let us first examine the investment approaches we seek to replace.

Investment versus speculation

The distinction between investment and speculation has become blurred, particularly in recent years as yesterday's concepts have become today's misconceptions. How is an investor, particularly a beginner, to know the difference? Graham and Dodd's *Security Analysis*, written in 1934, attempted a precise formulation of the difference between the terms *investment* and *speculation:* "An investment operation is one which, upon thorough analysis, promises safety of principal and an adequate return. Operations not meeting these requirements are speculative."[1]

Later, in his best seller, *The Intelligent Investor*, Benjamin Graham expressed concern about the radical changes that had taken place in the use of the term *investment* since he first formulated its definition.[2] He stated:

---

[1] Benjamin Graham, David L. Dodd, Sidney Cottle, and Charles Tatham, *Security Analysis*, 4th ed. (New York: McGraw-Hill, 1962).

[2] Benjamin Graham, *The Intelligent Investor*, 5th ed. (New York: Harper & Row, 1973).

> After the great market decline of 1929-32 all common stocks were widely regarded as speculative by nature. (A leading authority stated flatly that only bonds could be bought for investment.) Thus we had to defend our definition against the charge that it gave too wide a scope to the concept of investment. . . . Now our concern is of the opposite sort. We must prevent our readers from accepting the common jargon which applies the term "investor" to anybody and everybody in the stock market.

Ironically, the reverse was probably true: a good investment would have been the 1929-32 stock market; and stock purchases in the mid-1960s were based on a kind of buying hysteria.

If Graham were alive today, he would most likely expand his concern to include anybody and everybody "investing" in commodity futures, put and call options, postage stamps, gems, Chinese ceramics, and bubble gum cards. I accept Graham's definition of the term *investment* without hesitation. Whenever I use the term, it will pertain to conservative strategies within the framework of our nation's capital markets. This book was written solely for *investors* seeking superior alternatives to traditional investment strategies.

Traditional investment strategies

Our capital markets offer a variety of choices. They commonly include the following traditional investment instruments:

1. *U.S. government Treasury bills* (or other cash substitutes like bank certificates of deposit and commercial paper): purchased in large increments by investors seeking extremely liquid, risk-free interest. The rate of return will vary with short-term interest rates. Money market mutual funds fit this category and offer the advantages of purchase in small increments, check-writing privileges, and safety through diversification.
2. *U.S. government bonds:* purchased by investors desiring a higher long-term yield than Treasury bills and willing to accept fluctuations in market value as long-term interest rates rise or fall during the life of the bond.

3. *Corporate bonds:* purchased by investors wanting higher income than that provided by government bonds and willing to accept the additional risk of possible default by the issuing corporation. For investors in high income tax brackets (individuals or corporations), tax-exempt municipal bonds may be appropriate substitutes for corporate bonds.

4. *Common stocks:* purchased by investors striving for higher total returns (income plus capital appreciation) than what can be derived from corporate bonds and who are willing to accept even greater market fluctuations. Typical portfolios of good-quality common stocks should generally behave in accordance with traditional market measurement standards like the Dow Jones Industrial Average of 30 stocks or the Standard & Poor's 500 Composite Index (S&P 500). Other averages and indexes are available, but most are heavily influenced by speculative stocks that are outside the definition of the term *investment.*

Since I will frequently refer to stock market alternatives throughout this book, it is necessary to have a means for comparing them with the market. I have chosen the S&P 500 as my stock market proxy. This index is a broader bench mark of common stock performance than the Dow. It includes 500 of the largest stock issues having a total value of nearly $1 trillion; and because each stock is weighted by its market value, the index reasonably reflects the aggregate returns from the total U.S. stock market. The S&P 500 has also outperformed the Dow in recent years, thus it provides a more difficult challenge to the strategies I will be presenting.

The following performance data for the four investment alternatives discussed above are the courtesy of *Stocks, Bonds, Bills and Inflation: Historical Returns,* by Ibbotson and Sinquefield.[3] Results for the 55-year period from 1926 through 1980 are presented in Table 1. The consumer price index, as a measurement of inflation, is also included for comparison.

Investors often conclude that the few extra percentage points that might be earned from a common stock portfolio are not

---

[3] Roger G. Ibbotson and Rex A. Sinquefield, *Stocks, Bonds, Bills and Inflation: Historical Returns,* 2d ed. (Charlottesville, Va.: The Financial Analysts Research Foundation, 1979, with follow-up supplements).

TABLE 1
Annual compounded rates of return for traditional investment alternatives

	55 years 1926-80	10 years 1971-80	5 years 1976-80	1 year 1980
Consumer price index	2.9%	8.1%	9.2%	12.4%
Treasury bills	2.8	6.8	7.7	11.4
Government bonds	3.1	4.4	2.5	− 3.0
Corporate bonds*	3.7	4.2	2.4	− 2.6
Common stocks	9.4	8.4	14.0	32.5

*Based on the Salomon Brothers High-Grade Long-Term Corporate Bond Index.

worth the extra risk. This was especially true following the 1973-74 bear market when individuals and institutional investors alike withdrew from the stock market in droves. Assuming $1,000 were invested in each of the different alternatives in 1926 and left to compound for 55 years, tax free, the $1,000 investments would have grown to the following values at the end of 1980:

Treasury bills . . . . $	4,600
Government bonds	5,100
Corporate bonds	7,300
Common stocks	141,000

The differences between the fixed income and the equity investments are phenomenal. After taxes, the advantage of common stocks would have been even greater because at least some of this return would have been in the form of long-term capital gain, which is preferable to ordinary income. The stock market has been, by far, the best alternative for long-term investment funds, provided one was willing and able to withstand occasional shocks along the way. For example, the S&P 500 index declined over 70 percent in less than three years from its 1929 peak (dividends included). More recently, the index dropped over 40 percent during the 1973-74 bear market.

Until fairly recently, bonds were considered relatively immune to such catastrophic events. This picture changed drastically during the years leading up to the preparation of this book. Over the four-year period from 1977 through 1980, the Salomon Brothers Corporate Bond Index declined by 5 percent, *including reinvestment of interest*, while the consumer price index soared nearly 50 percent. Tax-exempts were hit even harder—as witness the Standard & Poor's municipal bond index, which dropped over 16 percent. Adjusted for inflation, this bond market debacle was nearly as devastating as the great stock market crash of the early 30s.

However, the S&P 500 stock index kept pace with inflation by posting a gain of more than 50 percent for this four-year period. We are now seeing articles in the financial press questioning the viability of the bond market as an investment arena for our nation's pension funds and for other conservative investors.

It should be clear by now that I believe the "truths" we accept without question are often dead wrong. As you read this book I ask you to go back to the basics and reexamine your own beliefs about investing and the market. Thoughtful skepticism is a trait which, I suspect, is shared by all successful investors.

The capital market line

Is there any easy-to-understand method of relating risk to reward for the purpose of making decisions? The investment community portrays long-term risk-reward relationships for various investment strategies through the capital market line. Exhibit 1 graphically displays the information given in Table 1: the comparative returns for various investment alternatives over a 55-year period. The vertical axis shows the average rate of return while the horizontal axis indicates relative risk. Notice that the capital market line intersects the vertical axis at the zero-risk level (a portfolio of risk-free Treasury bills). As risk is increased, the return also increases.

For conservative investors, the upper region of the line is representative of a good-quality common stock portfolio, much like the S&P 500 index. However, investors will usually have a combination portfolio of common stocks and bonds (or short-term money market instruments). A portfolio apportioned equally by dollars

EXHIBIT 1
The capital market line (55-year data, 1926-1980)

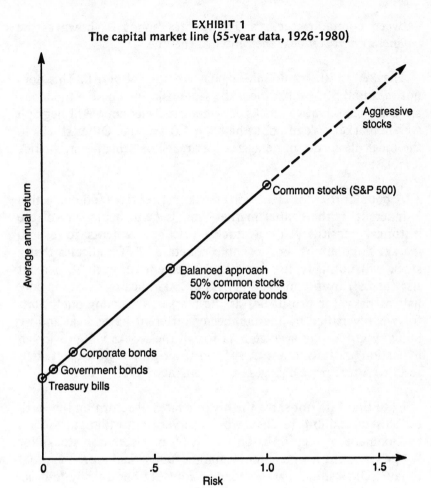

between common stocks and corporate bonds is shown as the *balanced approach* near the center of the line.

The S&P 500, by definition, has a risk level of 1.0. This does not mean all 500 stocks incur the same risk. Included in the index are such conservative stocks as American Telephone & Telegraph with a market risk of about half the 1.0 average. Other stocks in the index lie in the more aggressive area shown higher on the risk level line.

A popular tool for identifying stock market risk (and one which is inherent in the capital market line) is *beta:* a measure of the historical sensitivity of a stock's price movements to overall market fluctuations. For example, a beta of 1.50 indicates that a stock will normally rise (or fall) 15 percent for each 10 percent rise (or fall) by the market. A beta of .50 indicates a stock is only half as risky (or profitable) as the market. Assuming one's portfolio is diversified by the number of different issues held and by industry groups, an average beta for all the stocks will provide an indication of how one's overall portfolio might be expected to react to future price changes in the general market.

Note that I do not show the historic rates of return on the vertical axis of Exhibit 1. They would be very misleading in today's environment of high inflation (e.g., why buy common stocks for 9.4 percent return when money market funds yield more than that today?) Our capital markets tend to adjust rather quickly to inflationary changes. For example, as the consumer price index advanced over 12 percent during 1980, the yields on both Treasury bills and high-quality corporate bonds rose to over 14 percent and the stock market gained over 30 percent. Thus we can expect the capital market line to shift up or down with inflationary changes. But the relationships between points on the line should remain unchanged through these fluctuations. The Treasury bill rate of return in the future should roughly equal increases in the consumer price index, as has been historically true, and the returns for other investments should adjust accordingly.

All markets will continue to fluctuate, of course, and in recent years the stock market has been extremely sensitive to changes in short-term interest rates. But be wary of the money market trap; investors who attempt to capture the peak rates for risk-free money market instruments by shifting out of the stock market are usually disappointed because high short-term rates generally coincide with stock market bottoms. Many investors withdraw from stocks at the worst possible times, then reenter the stock market later after substantial price advances have taken place, and thus are whipsawed during the process. *Investors* should design their portfolios for optimum long-term performance and not worry about short-term market swings.

The least understood securities

In his excellent book, *The Money Masters,* John Train stated:

Benjamin Graham ranks as this century's (and perhaps history's) most important thinker on applied portfolio investment ... the best book ever written for the stockholder is *The Intelligent Investor.* One is ill-advised to the point of folly to buy a bond or a share of stock without having read its three hundred pages ... yet, alas, few stockbrokers, let alone investors, have done it.[4]

I certainly agree with Train that Benjamin Graham was an outstanding market tactician who imparted sound advice to his readers. In *The Intelligent Investor,* for example, he counseled his readers to apportion their assets between high-quality bonds and blue-chip common stocks. He warned against fads, new issues, trading techniques, and other "exciting" but unprofitable strategies.

However, Graham also was suspicious of "exotic" securities, including convertible bonds. He advised that convertibles were seldom mathematically attractive and should be avoided by most investors. Since most investors *are not* informed about convertibles (even most intelligent investors), I agree they should avoid this specialized area of the market—as they should avoid any investment area where they lack the necessary training. I also agree that investors should not buy convertibles that are mathematically unattractive. Serious investors, however, can acquire the knowl-

---

[4] John Train, *The Money Masters,* (New York: Harper & Row, 1980).

edge and skills necessary for searching out convertibles that are indeed attractive. This book is designed to teach you how.

I have spent my entire investment career specializing in convertible bonds and other exotic securities that are not well understood by the investment community. My activities have included writing books, managing client assets by employing strategies which use these securities, conducting investment conferences, and maintaining an ongoing discussion with other market professionals. One basic observation I draw from my experience is: The vast majority of investors, intelligent individuals and professional money managers alike, simply don't understand convertibles. They haven't spent the time and effort needed to learn the subject. Their broad avoidance of the convertible market has helped to create opportunities that have been truly unbelievable, and I see no trend to the contrary. I expect, in the foreseeable future, that the convertible securities market will continue to offer knowledgeable investors the opportunity to substantially tip the odds in their favor.

This book will present strategies involving *carefully selected* convertible securities that can be far more profitable than the traditional investments of Exhibit 1. These convertible strategies can be categorized as follows:

1. *Aggressive convertibles:* an alternative to good quality common stocks.
2. *Low-risk convertibles:* an alternative to the balanced approach of stocks and bonds.
3. *Convertible hedging:* alternatives to bonds and Treasury bills.

My objective is to convince you to pursue one or more of these convertible strategies instead of the stocks, bonds, or money market instruments that you may presently own.

My methodology will include the techniques for identifying superior opportunities, risk-reward analysis, portfolio management tactics, and, where meaningful, examples from my investment experience.

As I will demonstrate, you can expect to earn rates of return *well above* those of traditional investments. Higher return on your investment will certainly be worth the time and effort spent in mastering the subject. In addition, you will receive the immeasurable satisfaction of knowing you can beat the pros in the largest and most challenging investment arena in the world, the U.S. securities market.

CHAPTER 1

Introduction to convertible bonds

Convertible bonds (debentures) are a popular financing vehicle, born when they suit the issuing company's purpose. This generally occurs during periods of high interest rates and when its common stock is in vogue. Under such conditions, for example, if a company had to pay 14 percent to sell its straight debt, it might be able to issue a convertible debenture for only 8 percent. The company gains this cost advantage by sweetening the deal with what can be termed a *stock-purchase option* on its common stock which is "combined" with a straight bond to form the convertible. The option is exercisable anytime during the life of the bond, usually 20 years or more. It is the company's hope the bond will eventually be converted into common as its stock price rises in the future.

Like a straight (nonconvertible) corporate bond, a convertible bond provides a fixed payment of interest (coupon) and a maturity date when the issuing company must repay the principal (usually $1,000). However, a convertible offers an additional advantage to the bondholder. It may be exchanged (converted) for a specified number of shares of common stock. The higher the stock's price, the more valuable the convertible bond becomes. In essence these hybrid securities offer investors a combination of benefits similar to a balanced portfolio of common stocks and straight corporate bonds.

Since much of a convertible bond's attractiveness to investors is the possibility for capital gains if the underlying common stock rises, it is easier to market when the common stock is in favor. The number of convertibles has dramatically increased as the more glamorous companies continue to choose this low-cost way of borrowing. During 1980, for instance, many new convertibles in popular groups like energy, computers, and brokerage firms were issued. Over time, convertibles representing a broad cross section of the overall stock market have become available. Table 1-1 presents a list of 100 bonds that were actively traded on the New York or American Stock Exchange in mid-1981. As you scan the list, I am sure you will recognize most of the names. It is incorrectly assumed, by many who reject convertibles, that convertibles are brought to market only by low-quality corporations.

As a general rule, most convertible bonds offer both higher yield than their common stocks and less risk if the stocks decline in

TABLE 1-1
Actively traded convertible bonds, July 1981

Company	Bond description*
Allied Corp.	7.75 -05
ARA Services	4.625-96
American Airlines	5.25 -98
American Medical Int'l.	8.00 -00
Amfac	5.25 -94
Anheuser-Busch	9.00 -05
Avco	5.50 -93
Bally Manufacturing	6.00 -98
Bank New York	6.25 -94
BankAmerica Realty Inv.	9.50 -00
Bard (C.R.)	4.25 -96
Baxter Travenol Labs	4.75 -01
Becton Dickinson	5.00 -89
Burlington Industries	5.00 -91
Caterpillar Tractor	5.50 -00
Celanese	9.75 -06
Cenco	5.00 -96
Chase Manhattan	6.50 -96
Chemical New York	5.00 -93
Citicorp	5.75 -00
City Investing	7.50 -90
Columbia Pictures	9.50 -05
Computer Sciences	6.00 -94
Conn. General Mtg. & Realty	6.00 -96
Dayco	6.00 -94
Dean Witter Reynolds	10.00 -05
Dorchester Gas	8.50 -05
Eastern Air Lines	11.75 -05
FMC Corp.	4.25 -92
Federal Nat'l. Mtg. Assn.	4.375-96
First Int'l. Bancshares	7.75 -05
First Union RE	10.00 -06
Fischbach	8.50 -05
Ford Motor	4.875-98
Foremost McKesson	9.75 -06
Fruehauf	5.50 -94
GATX Corp.	5.75 -99
General Amer. Oil Texas	8.50 -00
General Tel. & Electronics	5.00 -92
Georgia Pacific	5.25 -96
Grace (W.R.)	4.25 -90
Greyhound	6.50 -90
Grumman	11.00 -00

*Bonds are normally identified by their coupon and an abbreviated maturity date; for example, 7.75-05 means 7.75 percent (at $1,000 par value) maturing in the year 2005.

TABLE 1-1 *(continued)*

Company	Bond description*
Gulf States Utilities	7.25 -92
Gulf United	9.25 -05
Harte-Hanks Communications	8.00 -05
Hercules	6.50 -99
Heublein	4.50 -97
Holiday Inns	9.625-05
Houston Industries	5.50 -85
Hutton (E.F.)	9.50 -05
Inexco Oil	8.50 -00
International Tel. & Tel.	8.625-00
K mart	6.00 -99
Kaiser Cement	9.00 -05
Lockheed	4.25 -92
Lomas & Nettleton Fin'l.	5.50 -91
Mapco	10.00 -05
Mass Mutual Mtg. & Realty	6.25 -91
McDonnell Douglas	4.75 -91
Merrill Lynch	9.25 -05
Minn. Mining & Mfg.	4.25 -97
Morgan (J.P.)	4.75 -98
National Steel	4.625-94
North American Philips	4.00 -92
Northwest Bancorp.	6.75 -03
Norton	9.50 -05
Oak Industries	11.00 -00
Ogden	5.00 -93
Owens-Illinois	4.50 -92
Pan Amer. World Airways	7.50 -98
Pfizer	4.00 -97
Purex Industries	4.875-94
RCA Corp.	4.50 -92
Ralston Purina	5.75 -00
Revere Copper & Brass	5.50 -92
Rexnord	9.25 -05
Reynolds Metals	4.50 -91
SCM Corp.	5.50 -88
Sherwin Williams	6.25 -95
Signal Companies	5.50 -94
Southeast Banking	4.75 -97
Storage Technology	10.25 -00
Storer Broadcasting	8.50 -05
Texas Air	8.375-00
Tidewater	7.75 -05
Tiger International	8.625-05
Trans World	12.00 -05
United Brands	5.50 -94
U.S. Air	8.25 -05

TABLE 1-1 *(concluded)*

Company	Bond description*
U.S. Steel	5.75 -01
United Telecommunications	5.00 -93
Varian Associates	8.75 -05
Virginia Electric & Power	3.625-86
Walter, Jim	5.75 -91
Wang Labs	9.50 -05
Wells Fargo Mtg.	12.00 -05
Western Union	5.25 -97
Xerox	6.00 -95
Zenith Radio	8.375-05

price. *These are major advantages.* Other advantages are lower transaction costs, senior status in the company's financial structure compared to its common stock, and guaranteed income. The disadvantage is that most convertibles will not provide quite as much capital appreciation when their stocks advance in price. An easy-to-prepare risk-reward analysis for each convertible under consideration will enable you to identify those that are attractive alternatives to their common.

Criteria and procedures employed in the risk-reward analysis will be presented in the following chapter, but you must first understand the major elements that influence the price of a convertible bond: its investment value and its conversion value. *Study the next few pages carefully.* They will give you the important basics needed to understand the rest of the book.

Estimated investment value

A convertible bond's investment value is the price at which it would be expected to trade if it were a straight (nonconvertible) bond. This value is estimated by bond-rating services in the same way straight bonds are evaluated. The bond raters consider the inherent quality of the bond relative to prevailing interest rates for similar securities.

In recent years most investors in straight corporate bonds (or tax-exempts) have been surprised, if not shocked, as they saw market values plummet in response to rising interest rates. Table 1-2 illustrates the relationship between investment value and prevailing interest rates for a typical bond (convertible or nonconvertible) having an 8 percent coupon and a 20-year life.

TABLE 1-2
Investment value for an 8 percent, 20-year
bond versus prevailing long-term interest rates

Prevailing long-term interest rate	Investment value
8%	$1,000
10	830
12	700
14	600
16	525
18	465
20	415

Note: Bonds are evaluated and traded in terms of their yield-to-maturity values. Refer to the tables of a *yield book* to determine the precise yield-to-maturity for a given coupon, maturity date, and market price.

If straight bonds of similar quality were yielding 14 percent to maturity, an investment value of $600 would be assigned to a hypothetical 8 percent, 20-year convertible of XYZ Company (Table 1-2). This figure is shown as the horizontal line of Exhibit 1-1 and is the first step toward preparing a risk-reward analysis. Note that bond prices, shown on the vertical axis of the exhibit, are expressed as a percent of par. Thus 60 (dollar sign intentionally omitted) means 60 percent of $1,000 or $600. From this point on, I will use this traditional shorthand when quoting bond prices.

Theoretically, the estimated investment value of 60 is independent of the stock's price shown on the horizontal axis. In the real world, however, if the stock price were to decline substantially, it would probably indicate deteriorating fundamentals. In that event, the investment values of all senior securities of a company, including its convertible bonds, might have to be downgraded.

EXHIBIT 1-1
Estimated investment value for XYZ Company 8 percent, 20-year
convertible bond (yield to maturity = 14 percent)

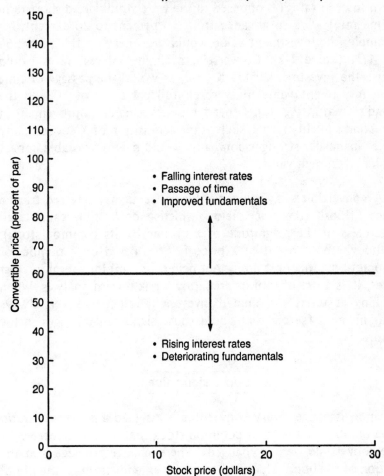

The impact of changing interest rates on the convertible's investment value is of more immediate concern. If prevailing long-term interest rates (as opposed to the widely publicized short-term prime rate) were to advance from 14 percent to 20 percent, for example, the investment value would drop nearly a third from 60 to 41½ (Table 1-2). Conversely, declining interest rates would cause the investment value to rise, as would the passage of time (the investment value must reach full par value of 100 on the bond's maturity date). Other factors causing an improvement in the bond's quality rating, such as the acquisition of XYZ Company by a financially stronger company, would have a favorable impact on its investment value.

A convertible's investment value is frequently referred to as a price "floor" (the price below which a convertible cannot fall regardless of the magnitude of a decline by its common stock). Although the concept of a price floor is based on a number of assumptions, the most important being constant long-term interest rates, it is a useful tool in preparing a risk-reward analysis. When looking at today's estimated investment value, however, always bear in mind factors that could cause significant changes in the future.

Conversion value

Upon issuance, every convertible is assigned a *conversion ratio* (the number of shares of common stock that would be received if the convertible were exchanged). The exchange privilege is at the option of the bondholder and normally extends through the life of the bond. The bond's *conversion value* is the conversion ratio multiplied by the current market price of the common. This calculation represents the convertible's worth if it were exchanged for shares of common stock and the shares were immediately sold.

Assuming a conversion ratio of 50 shares for the XYZ Company bond, the conversion value is shown as the sloping line of Exhibit 1-2. For example, if the stock were trading at $20 per share, the conversion value is 100 ($1,000):

50 shares X $20 per share = $1,000

EXHIBIT 1-2
Conversion value for XYZ Company 8 percent, 20-year
convertible bond (conversion ratio = 50 shares)

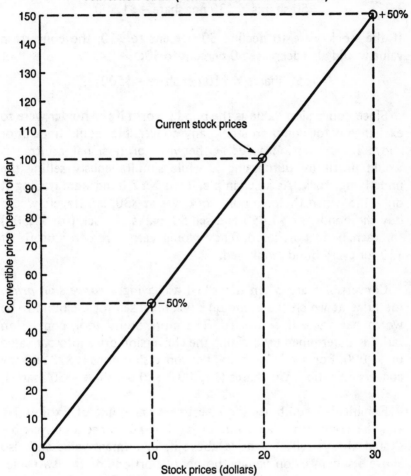

If the stock were to advance 50 percent to $30, the conversion value would also increase 50 percent to 150:

50 shares × $30 per share = $1,500

If the stock were to decline 50 percent to $10, the conversion value would also decrease 50 percent to 50:

50 shares × $10 per share = $500

Since conversion value is the bond's worth if the holder were to exchange it for common stock, any convertible should trade at or above its conversion value. Otherwise, professional arbitragers would profit by purchasing it while simultaneously selling the underlying stock. As an example, if the XYZ bond were trading at only 145 when the common stock was at $30, arbitragers would buy the bonds for $1,450 and sell 50 shares of stock (for $1,500) for each bond purchased. They would earn a risk-free profit of $50 for every bond purchased.

Convertibles are often described as having a *conversion price,* the price at which the common stock must sell for the bond to be worth par value if converted. The more useful tool, conversion ratio, is determined by dividing the conversion price into par value of $1,000. For XYZ Company, the conversion price is $20 and the conversion ratio is 50 shares ($1,000 ÷ $20 per share = 50 shares).

Exhibit 1-3 combines the investment value line of Exhibit 1-1 and the conversion value line of Exhibit 1-2. Since a convertible should always sell at a price above its investment value and also above its conversion value, the heavy portions of the two lines represent minimum bond prices relative to all future stock prices.

The convertible price curve

Exhibit 1-4 repeats the investment value and conversion value lines of Exhibit 1-3 and introduces the concept of a *convertible price curve:* a curve showing the *expected* convertible price for any stock price over the near-term future.

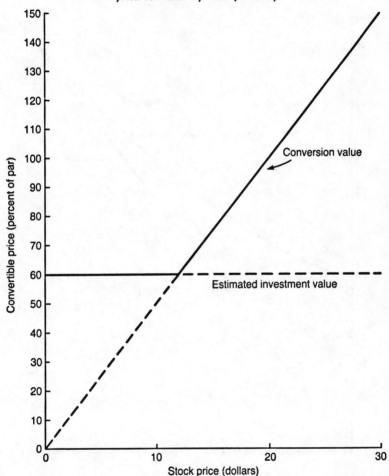

EXHIBIT 1-3
Price boundaries for XYZ Company 8 percent, 20-year
convertible bond (conversion ratio = 50 shares;
yield-to-maturity = 14 percent)

EXHIBIT 1-4
The convertible price curve for XYZ Company 8 percent,
20-year convertible bond (conversion ratio = 50 shares;
yield-to-maturity = 14 percent)

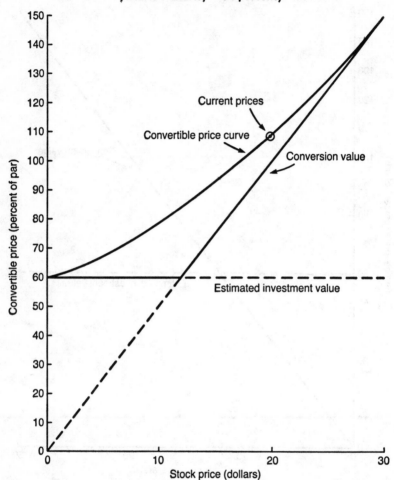

Academicians have attempted to describe the precise configuration of the convertible price curve with complex mathematical formulas. I applaud the efforts of those who seek the "precise formula" for modeling the curve; however, formulas are not a replacement for common sense. Any formula must be based on imprecise data, including one's estimate of the underlying common stock's future price volatility, plus an educated guess at what point the company might call the bond. Other factors important to "the formula," such as the bond's quality rating and the prevailing interest rate, are subject to rapid changes in the future.

Fortunately, a speedy way to approximate the curve that is sufficient for all practical purposes does exist. As displayed by Exhibit 1-4, the price curve passes through current market prices for the two securities, shown as 110 and $20 for the bond and stock, respectively. On the downside, the price curve reaches the investment value line marking another point on the curve, 60 at a stock price of $0. Both these points (110 versus $20 and 60 versus $0) must fall on any curve whether it is approximated or computed mathematically. A third point, necessary for modeling the curve, is more subjective. Here one's experience must be brought into play, recognizing that, as the convertible advances to well above par, most companies (but not all) will call their bonds, thereby forcing conversion. Thus at some high price level the bond's price must reach the conversion value line. I assumed this would occur at a price of 150 with the stock at $30. The convertible price curve of Exhibit 1-4 was drawn by connecting these three points with a French curve. This approach is sufficient for determining whether the convertible is a buy, hold, or sell candidate, as I will show in the next chapter.

Since the convertible price curve (defined above) must accommodate itself to transitory current prices, the curve changes every time current prices change. For example, if the bond were trading at 115 instead of 110 (with the stock still at $20) a different curve would result which passes through the common points of 60 versus $0 and 150 versus $30.

Preparation of the convertible price curve constitutes the final step leading to the risk-reward analysis presented in the next chapter. However, before proceeding, the balance of this chapter provides other tools that are useful for comprehensive analysis.

Premium over conversion value. A convertible's premium over conversion value (conversion premium) is a popular and important tool for measuring worth. When the conversion premium is low, a convertible will respond more readily to the moves of its common stock price. At a price of 110, with the underlying stock trading at $20, the XYZ Company bond's conversion premium is only 10 percent.

$$\text{Conversion value} = 50 \text{ shares} \times \$20 \text{ per share} = \$1,000$$

$$\text{Conversion premium} = \frac{\$1,100 - \$1,000}{\$1,000} = 10\%$$

Premium over investment value. A convertible's premium over investment value (investment value premium) is just as important as a conversion premium in the risk-reward analysis. When the investment value premium is low, the convertible is less likely to drop sharply upon a price decline by its common stock. This term is infrequently mentioned in the financial press or by most investment advisory services specializing in convertibles. They seldom evaluate the *risk* of their recommendations. The XYZ Company bond's investment value premium is a relatively high 83 percent.

$$\text{Investment value} = \$600$$

$$\text{Investment value premium} = \frac{\$1,100 - \$600}{\$600} = 83\%$$

Yield advantage. Assuming XYZ Company common stock pays annual dividends of $1 per share, the current yield advantage for the convertible is 2.3 percent.

$$\text{Convertible bond yield} = \frac{\$80}{\$1,100} = 7.3\%$$

$$\text{Minus stock yield} = \frac{\$1}{\$20} = \underline{-5.0}$$

$$\text{Yield advantage} = 2.3\%$$

Most new convertibles provide yield advantages over their underlying common stocks. As time passes, the advantage will diminish if the stock's dividend is increased, since the convertible's cash payout remains fixed throughout the life of the bond.

Break-even time. Another analytical tool is the number of years it will take for the convertible's yield advantage to make up for its present premium over conversion value. The break-even time for the XYZ Company bond is 4.3 years.

$$\text{Break-even time} = \frac{10\% \text{ Conversion premium}}{2.3\% \text{ Yield advantage}} = 4.3 \text{ Years}$$

Break-even time is probably the most popular tool employed by most professional convertible buyers. Institutional money managers look for recovery of the conversion premium in about three years. However, convertibles having very long break-even times may be superior alternatives to their common stocks if there is any possibility that the stock's dividend may be reduced. For the same reason, some convertibles are a better alternative even when their yields are below those of their stocks. Ford Motor and Federal National Mortgage bonds were good examples of this situation in 1980. Both convertibles were yielding less than their common stocks and could have been purchased exactly at their conversion values. When the companies cut their stock dividends in half, the convertibles immediately went to premiums above conversion values, reflecting their new yield advantages. The extra income safety provided by the bonds as senior securities made them better investments than their common stocks, even at negative yield advantages.

Convertible preferreds

Unlike convertible bonds, which are instruments companies use primarily to attain new financing, convertible preferreds usually come to the market via mergers or acquisitions. The shareholders of the company being acquired do not have an immediate tax liability if they receive new preferred stock or common stock (equity securities) in exchange for their original common shares. (If they receive cash or debt instruments, including convertible bonds, their original shares would be treated as having been sold.) Since the company being acquired is usually in a position to strike a hard bargain, it negotiates a higher-yielding and higher-quality convertible preferred in lieu of common. The disadvantage to the company issuing the preferred is that dividends are paid from aftertax profits, whereas bond interest is fully tax deductible to the corporation.[1]

Since convertible bonds and convertible preferreds have many similar characteristics, both may be evaluated on such factors as conversion premium, investment value premium, and yield advantage. Yet, there are significant differences which may influence investment strategy.

Claim on assets. Since bondholder claims on a company's assets are senior to those of preferred stockholders, bonds are inherently safer: a distinction of minor consequence if the company is financially sound. It is of major importance when considering convertibles of a speculative company.

Continuity of payments. The failure of a company to meet bond-interest obligations places it in default and is the first step toward bankruptcy. Since preferred dividends are seldom guaranteed, a company will suspend dividends on its preferred stock, during adverse times, before discontinuing bond interest payments. Even though the dividends paid on preferred stock are usually cumulative (arrearages must be made up before any dividends can be paid to common shareholders), holders of preferred stock may have a long wait before receiving the dividends once the dividends are suspended. Eventually, preferred stock shareholders may even have to accept some sort of exchange offer from the company, in lieu of bankruptcy, and may never see the dividend arrearages paid.

Tax consequences. Dividends received from preferred or common stocks possess unique tax advantages to corporations *buying* these securities. Whereas bond interest is fully taxable as ordinary income, corporations are permitted to exclude 85 percent of the dividends received from most preferreds and common stocks. These tax benefits to corporate investors historically have kept the

---

[1] In spite of the adverse tax consequences, preferred stock sometimes must be used for new financing to maintain a proper balance between the corporation's debt and equity.

yields of preferreds slightly lower than those of bonds in spite of the greater safety of the bond; thus individual investors or pension funds should usually buy higher-yielding, higher-quality bonds instead of preferreds.

Maturity date. Since bonds have a fixed maturity date, ultimately they must be redeemed by the company at par value. An approaching maturity date provides protection against price weakness caused by rising interest rates. It also may protect the convertible bond against a serious price decline by the common stock without limiting its potential appreciation. Preferred stocks, which

TABLE 1-3
Actively traded convertible preferreds, July 1981

Company	Preferred description*	Company	Preferred description*
AMAX	$3.00	Georgia Pacific	$2.24A
Amerada Hess	3.50	Gulf & Western	2.50
American Brands	2.67	Gulf United	3.78
American Tel. & Tel.	4.00	Heinz (H.J.)	1.70
Arcata	2.16	Household International	2.50
Armco	2.10	IC Industries	3.50
Atlantic Richfield	2.80	Ingersoll Rand	2.35
Beatrice Foods	3.38	International Harvester	5.76
Bendix	4.04	International Tel. & Tel.	4.00K
Bristol-Myers	2.00	Jewel Co's.	2.31
Brunswick	2.40	Libbey-Owens-Ford	4.75
Carter Hawley Hale	2.00	McDermott	2.20
Champion International	4.60	Natomas	4.00
Chemical New York	1.875	Pennwalt	1.60
Chromalloy American	5.00	Pitney-Bowes	2.12
City Investing	2.00	RCA Corp.	2.125
Consolidated Foods	4.50	Sun Co.	2.25
Continental Group	2.00	Tesoro Petroleum	2.16
Cooper Industries	2.90	Textron	2.08
Crocker National	2.1875	Time Inc.	1.575
Crown Zellerbach	4.625	United States Gypsum	1.80
Diamond International	1.20	United Technologies	2.55
FMC Corp.	2.25	Weyerhaeuser	2.80
GAF Corp.	1.20	Wheelabrator-Frye	4.125
General Dynamics	4.25	Woolworth (F.W.)	2.20

*Preferred stocks are normally identified by their annual dividend payments. If two different issues carry the same dividend, letters are added to distinguish the differences (e.g., $2.00 pfd A and $2.00 pfd B).

seldom have a maturity date, are more sensitive to changing market conditions.

Table 1-3 presents a representative list of 50 convertible preferreds that were actively traded on the New York Stock Exchange in mid-1981. I am sure you will recognize most of the names of these major corporations.

Special situations

Up to this point I have described conventional convertible bonds and preferreds that are immediately exchangeable into common shares at any time throughout the life of the convertible. These represent the largest part of the convertible securities market. Yet, there are unusual convertibles that may offer either greater opportunities for the alert investor or hidden traps for the unwary. All investors should be able to evaluate these special situations. They are presented in Appendix A, following this chapter.

The next two chapters will provide important guidelines for evaluating candidates and for building and managing a portfolio of convertibles. Before proceeding, however, I urge you to master the basic concepts and terms presented this far. This will facilitate understanding subsequent chapters.

APPENDIX A

Special convertibles

The following discourse presents special convertibles that I have employed in the past. We may expect to see different ones in the future, as corporate treasurers strain their imaginations, during periods difficult for new financing via conventional securities.

Plus-cash convertible. This security requires an additional cash payment on conversion. Since the cash payment is constant regardless of the common stock's market price, the conversion value changes faster than the price of the underlying stock. This type of special convertible may be of interest to investors seeking greater leverage than that offered by conventional convertibles.

An example is the United Air Lines (UAL) 4¼s of 1992, exchangeable into 19 common shares upon payment of $260. With the common stock at $20 in early 1981, the bond's conversion value was only $120, calculated as follows:

Conversion value = 19 shares X $20 per share minus $260
= $380 − $260
= $120

If the common stock were to double to $40, the conversion value would increase by more than 300 percent to $500.

Conversion value = 19 shares X $40 per share minus $260
= $760 − $260
= $500

Unit convertible. Instead of being exchangeable only into common stock, such an issue is convertible into a "unit"—a package of one or more securities that may or may not include the common. The evaluation of this convertible requires additional expertise, but a unit convertible is potentially more rewarding since the marketplace may have extra difficulty assigning it a fair value.

An example of a (currently unattractive) unit convertible, the Investors Diversified Services 6½s of 1992, is convertible into 21.5 units, each unit consisting of one share of Alleghany Corporation's $2.86 nonconvertible preferred and a half share of Alleghany common. These terms resulted from Alleghany's acquisition of IDS in 1980.

Indirect convertible. This security may be exchanged into common stock via another convertible. For example, the Instrument Systems 12s of 1999 is convertible into 90 shares of a preferred stock, which in turn is convertible into 10 shares of common. Since the preferred pays a very small dividend, its price action is directly related to the common. The bond may therefore be evaluated as being convertible into 900 shares of common stock. Other indirect convertibles may require greater study when evaluating their risk-reward characteristics.

Fabricated convertible. This special convertible is a combination of warrants plus straight bonds; bonds that may be used (at par value, $1,000) in lieu of the cash exercise price when exercising the warrants. To determine the number of warrants that should be purchased with each straight bond, simply divide the $1,000 par value of the bond by the exercise price of the warrant. The combination results in risk-reward characteristics similar to conventional convertibles, yet it provides greater flexibility as the bonds and warrants are purchased and sold separately. This was a popular form of financing in the go-go days of the 60s when warrents were in vogue. Its popularity declined during the 70s, but there are indications that warrants are again returning to favor.

A recent issue was brought to the market by Caesars World. Their 12½s of 2000 straight bond is usable when exercising their warrants that expire in August 1985. To fabricate a Caesars World convertible the investor should purchase 41 warrants along with each bond ($1,000 ÷ $24.50 warrant exercise price = 40.8 warrants).

Synthetic convertible. By combining call options (or warrants) with money market instruments, investors create synthetic convertible securities. This technique can be a profitable alternative to owning common stock when short-term interest rates are high and calls are undervalued. By placing most of the investment capital in high-yielding money market instruments and the small balance in call options, the synthetic convertible may offer stock market opportunity at a lower risk level than owning common stocks. Some investors, for example, routinely buy calls with 10 percent of their funds while holding 90 percent in the money market.

Delayed convertible. This convertible has delayed conversion features and generally sells at a discount below its future conversion value. A delayed convertible will usually fall into either of two categories:

1. A convertible with fixed conversion terms specifying the number of common stock shares to be received upon conversion commencing on a specified future date.
2. A convertible exchangeable into common stock beginning on a specified date: with the conversion ratio based upon a formula relating to the future price of the common.

All convertibles, conventional and special, may contain unusual terms requiring careful consideration or confront market conditions that may cause abnormal price action.

Changes in terms. Some convertibles have fixed schedules for changing their conversion terms at future specified dates. These changes usually involve a reduction of the conversion ratio, possibly subjecting the convertible to downward price pressure as the date nears.

The El Paso Natural Gas (El Paso Co.) 6s of 1993, for example, will experience an abrupt reduction of its conversion ratio from 59.03 shares to 50.98 shares on February 1, 1985. Depending on the bond's price at that time, conversion may be necessary to avoid a significant loss of value. If the bond were trading at its conversion value of 150, for example, it would drop to about 130.

Expiration of conversion privileges. An even more dangerous situation than a reduction of the conversion ratio is termination of conversion privileges. If this happens, the convertible's market price should immediately drop to its investment value as it loses its entire conversion privilege.

Current examples include the American Airlines 5¼s of 1998 on which conversion privileges terminate 12-15-83 and the United Air Lines 4¼s of 1992 which terminate 7-1-82. Assuming these bonds are trading above their investment values as the termination dates near, they must be sold or converted to avoid serious losses.

Call provisions. Practically all convertible bonds, and most convertible preferreds, may be redeemed by the company (like straight bonds and preferreds). For bonds, the call price is usually several points over its face value (e.g., $1,050). Companies that issue convertibles generally will redeem them when, due to a significant common stock rally, the convertible is much higher. If a convertible is subject to being called in the near future, be careful not to pay much of a premium over conversion value; when called, the convertible will immediately drop to its conversion value and the premium be lost.

Note that companies normally do not call convertibles with the intention of redeeming them for cash. Their usual objective is to force conversion into common stock to improve their balance sheet (or reduce their tax liabilities if the common stock is a low dividend payer). They therefore must be cautious in timing the call because subsequent market action by their common stock might force them to come up with cash they may not have. For example, if a bond's call price were 105 and it was trading at its conversion value of 110, the company would probably not issue a call because a small price decline by its common at any time up to the call date (usually thirty days later) might reduce the conversion value to below the call price. Bondholders would then redeem for cash rather than convert.

Note also that companies often will call a bond just prior to its interest payment date and save a considerable amount of money. The accrued interest must be added to the call price; but interest is not received if bondholders are forced to convert. For this reason, convertible bonds will decline to a discount below conversion value, when called, to reflect the loss of accrued interest (accrued interest is added to the purchase price which the new owner will never recover if the bond is converted).

Antidilution provisions. Convertibles almost always are protected against stock splits, stock dividends, and the like via an increase in their conversion ratios. However, there have been instances where a company has spun off a subsidiary to holders of its common stock without adjusting the conversion terms of its convertibles. We probably are unable to protect ourselves against such deceitful, if rare, tactics.

Sinking fund convertibles. Some convertible bonds and preferreds have sinking fund provisions that will retire much of the issue prior to the maturity date. Once the sinking fund redemptions begin, the convertible will start to behave like a short-term bond, one nearing its maturity date.

Other convertibles may have characteristics that are similar to a sinking fund. The Georgia Pacific $2.24 pfd A, for example, is scheduled to be redeemed at $39 over a five-year period starting 4-1-84. However, the company may choose not to redeem, in which event it must increase the preferred's annual dividend to $4.00.

Preferreds in arrears. Most companies are required to pay omitted past dividends on their preferred stocks before paying any future dividends on their common stock. These "cumulative" preferreds can build up very large dividend arrearages over a period of years and thus offer the potential for large payouts should the company regain profitability.

Tender offers for discounted bonds. Bonds are carried on a corporation's balance sheet as a liability at full par value. In an effort to improve its balance sheet, a company may make a cash tender or exchange offer for its deep-discounted bonds. The value offered is usually well above the current market price of the bond to assure a favorable response.

Mergers and tender offers for common stock. These events may have either positive or negative impact on the market value of a convertible, depending on the specific terms of the package offered to the common stockholders and the convertible's premium over conversion value.

The most dangerous—and unfair—situation occurs when a company is acquired for low-volatility securities (e.g., bonds or preferreds) or cash. To a large extent, the conversion premium reflects the possibility that the underlying common stock may make a meaningful price advance sometime in the future. Convertibles are normally protected in the event of a merger since holders receive the same terms that are offered to the common stockholders. When common stock of the acquiring company is received in a merger, it would be considered fair compensation because the convertible may then be exchangeable into the new common. However, if other low-volatility securities are received, the convertible could be adversely affected.

United Technologies, for example, acquired Carrier Corporation by issuing new shares of a convertible preferred stock. As a result, the Carrier $5\frac{1}{8}$s of 1989 became convertible into the new United Technologies preferred having much lower volatility than the Carrier common stock. The bond immediately lost its conversion premium and, in effect, the bondholders were forced to exchange their bonds for the higher-yielding preferred having a market value below the bond's call price.

These are some of the pluses and minuses I have experienced in working with convertible securities. In the future there will certainly be new and different ones. Through careful attention to detail, alert investors should be able to avoid most traps and to profit from the unusual opportunities that often arise.

Since unexpected events may occur, I recommend that investors do not keep convertible securities in their safety deposit boxes but rather in an account at a brokerage firm. Brokerage firms are alert to these happenings and send notices when action is necessary.

CHAPTER 2

Risk-reward analysis

Determining whether the convertible is an attractive alternative to its underlying stock (or to a stock/bond combination), requires the preparation of a *risk-reward analysis.*

I have repeated the estimated price curve for the XYZ Company convertible bond from the previous chapter as part of Exhibit 2-1 for your convenience. Note that the expected convertible bond prices for stock price moves of 25 and 50 percent in both directions from the stock's current price of $20 are highlighted. We can now evaluate the XYZ convertible, relative to its common stock, over the price range of $10 to $30 per share.

Table 2-1 presents the risk-reward analysis assuming a 12-month holding period. Note that stock dividends and bond interest are included in the net profit or loss figures. In this example, the convertible provides a typical yield advantage of 2 percent. Convertibles are available on stocks that do not pay a dividend and others yield less than their common. I will later demonstrate how a large yield advantage can significantly improve the merits of a convertible security relative to its underlying common.

Risk-reward advantage

An evaluation of the risk-reward analysis of Table 2-1 shows that the XYZ Company convertible bond offers about four fifths the upside potential of the common (43 percent versus 55 percent) at about half the downside risk (−22 percent versus −45 percent). This would seem to indicate a definite edge over its common stock, or, at the very least, an edge over some combination of common and straight bonds. In the past, I described this edge as a *risk-reward advantage* (RRA) relative to the common stock, and used it when the convertible was trading at a conversion premium of about 10 percent or less (recognizing that most convertibles are hybrid securities having investment characteristics relating to both stocks and bonds). Assuming stock price moves of plus or minus 50 percent, the RRA is calculated as follows:

EXHIBIT 2-1
The convertible price curve for XYZ Company 8 percent, 20-year
convertible bond (conversion ratio = 50 shares;
yield-to-maturity = 14 percent)

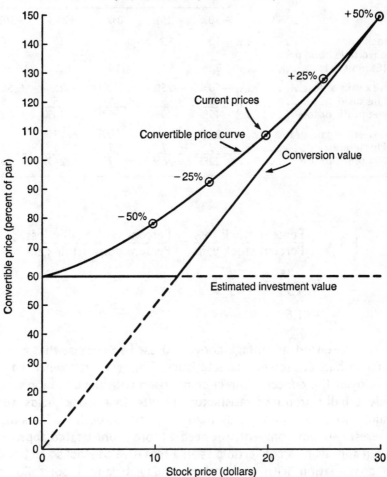

TABLE 2-1
Risk-reward analysis for XYZ Company 8 percent, 20-year convertible bond

	Assumed stock price change (next 12 months)				
	−50%	−25%	0%	+25%	+50%
Stock price	10	15	20	25	30
Convertible bond price					
(Exhibit 2-1)	78	93	110	129	150
Stock gain or loss	−50%	−25%	0%	+ 25%	+ 50%
Plus dividends	+ 5	+ 5	+ 5	+ 5	+ 5
Net profit or loss	−45%	−20%	+ 5%	+ 30%	+ 55%
Convertible gain or loss	−29%	−15%	0%	+ 17%	+ 36%
Plus interest	+ 7	+ 7	+ 7	+ 7	+ 7
Net profit or loss	−22%	− 8%	+ 7%	+ 24%	+ 43%

$$\text{RRA} = \frac{\text{Percent stock loss}}{\text{Percent stock gain}} \div \frac{\text{Percent convertible loss}}{\text{Percent convertible gain}}$$

$$= \frac{-45}{+55} \div \frac{-22}{+43}$$

$$= 1.6$$

A risk-reward advantage above 1.0 used to suggest that a convertible had attractive characteristics. This was true when I first employed the concept. Direct comparison with the common stock only usually produced satisfactory results since stock yields were much closer to bond yields than they are today. In today's high interest rate environment, we need a more sophisticated approach when appraising a convertible as an alternative to stocks and bonds in combination with each other. Today, balanced portfolios of stocks and bonds provide a higher-yield advantage over common stock portfolios. Thus, convertibles must provide correspondingly higher yields to offer comparable advantages.

Stock market equivalency and market advantage

Most convertibles should be viewed as an alternative to a combination of their underlying common stock and straight bonds.

The precise mix may be determined, and a *market advantage* (MA) calculation prepared. Assuming a constant long-term interest rate, over the next year, of 14 percent (equal to the yield on the convertible's investment value), total return estimates for 50 percent stock price moves are:

	Assumed stock price change (next 12 months)	
	−50%	+50%
XYZ common stock (Table 2-1)	−45%	+55%
XYZ convertible bond (Table 2-1)	−22%	+43%
XYZ straight bond	+14%	+14%

From these estimates, we can determine the mixture of common stock and straight bonds that entails the same risk as the convertible. Letting X represent the stock portion and Y the bond portion of the combination, calculations to solve for X are:

(Stock risk)X + (Bond return)Y = (Convertible risk)
since X + Y = 1, we can substitute (1 − X) for Y, thus
(Stock risk)X + (Bond return)(1 − X) = (Convertible risk)
(Stock risk)X + (Bond return) − (Bond return)X = (Convertible risk)
X(Stock risk − Bond return) = (Convertible risk) − (Bond return)

$$X = \frac{(\text{Convertible risk}) - (\text{Bond return})}{(\text{Stock risk}) - (\text{Bond return})}$$

$$= \frac{(-22) - (+14)}{(-45) - (+14)}$$

$$= \frac{-22 - 14}{-45 - 14}$$

$$= \frac{-36}{-59}$$

$$= .61$$

As determined from the above calculations, the convertible entails the same risk as a combination portfolio of 61 percent stock and 39 percent bonds. A convenient way to express this relationship is a *stock equivalency* (SE) of 61 percent. Future calculations for convertibles discussed in this book will use the following formula:

$$SE = \frac{(\text{Convertible risk}) - (\text{Bond return})}{(\text{Stock risk}) - (\text{Bond return})}$$

The convertible's market advantage would be its greater upside potential compared to the 61/39 combination, or it might offer a disadvantage if it provided less opportunity. Calculations are:

$$MA = \frac{(\text{Convertible return})}{.61(\text{Stock return}) + .39(\text{Bond return})}$$

$$= \frac{+43.0}{.61(+55) + .39(+14)}$$

$$= \frac{+43.0}{+33.6 + 5.5}$$

$$= \frac{+43.0}{+39.1}$$

$$= 1.1$$

A market advantage above 1.0 indicates that the convertible bond should be considered as having risk-reward characteristics superior to the calculated combination of common stock and straight bonds. When the advantages of a convertible are significant, I consider the market's pricing mechanism for that security to be inefficient. In other words, some convertible securities are *undervalued* relative to their underlying common stocks and straight bonds.

In the real world, not all convertibles are as attractive as the XYZ bond, while others are even better. Table 2-2 presents a sample list of 10 New York Stock Exchange bonds available in August 1981. As shown in the right-hand column, the market advantages for this group ranged from a low of .85 (Heublein) to a high of 1.32 (Storage Technology). The average MA is 1.11 for the 10 issues. However, as I will show in the the next chapter, carefully selected portfolios of undervalued convertibles can have MAs averaging near 1.5.

TABLE 2-2

Market advantages for a group of convertible bonds, August 1981

Company	Convertible description	Convertible price	Current yield		Leverage*		SE†	MA‡
			Stock	Convertible	−50%	+50%		
Avco	5.50 -93	67	4.5%	8.2%	−20%	+21%	44%	.91
Baxter Travenol Labs	4.375-91	143	3.1	1.4	−45	+50	89	1.13
City Investing	7.50 -90	160	6.0	4.7	−48	+50	99	.99
Federal Nat'l. Mortgage ...	4.375-96	56	2.0	7.8	−22	+24	48	.96
Heublein	4.50 -97	57	6.3	7.9	−18	−18	40	.85
Lockheed	4.25 -92	60	0	7.1	−21	+27	45	1.08
Mapco	10.00 -05	94	5.4	10.6	−14	+23	30	1.28
Storage Technology	9.00 -01	100	0	9.0	−19	+27	38	1.32
U.S. Air	8.25 -05	94	0.8	8.8	−23	+30	44	1.28
Zenith Radio	8.375-05	86	4.3	9.7	−18	+26	36	1.25
Averages			3.2%	7.5%	−25%	+30%	51%	1.11

*The projected percent change for the convertible for changes in the price of the underlying stock of −50 percent or +50 percent.

†Stock equivalency (SE) describes an alternative investment in common stock and straight bonds. The figure shown is the percent invested in stock (e.g., 45 percent means 45 percent stock and 55 percent straight bonds).

‡The market advantage (MA) indicates whether the convertible is undervalued (above 1.0) or overvalued (below 1.0) for stock price changes of −50 percent or +50 percent over a 12-month period.

Note that here and there throughout the book I chose price moves of 50 percent for calculating market advantages. Other combinations also may be used (e.g., −25 percent versus + 25 percent). However, I have found plus or minus 50 percent to be the most practical for ongoing comparisons of convertible securities since most stocks fluctuate over broad price ranges during 12-month periods.

Note also that MAs change as bond/stock price relationships change. For XYZ Company, the MA would drop to about .9 if the bond rose to 115 while the stock remained at $20. If the bond were to drop to 105 (with the common still at $20) the MA would be about 1.3. The market advantage is a useful calculation for making buy, hold, or sell decisions.

Interest rate risk

A convertible bond's future price is influenced by both the price action of its underlying common stock and the long-term interest rate fluctuations. Exhibit 2-2 shows expected price curves for the XYZ convertible for interest rates of 12 or 16 percent a year hence (as compared to the 14 percent prevailing rate for determining the investment value of Exhibit 2-1). The new investment values would be 70 at 12 percent and 52.5 at 16 percent (from Table 1-2 of Chapter 1).

As shown by the new price curves, interest rate changes would have little influence on the convertible's price if its stock were to advance (upside prices are controlled by the conversion value line, which cannot change). If the stock were to drop, a higher investment value would moderate the bond's price decline, or a lower investment value would add to its risk. In either event, the convertible bond's risk would be approximately that of the combination stock/straight bond portfolio (61 percent stock and 39 percent bonds).

The times when the XYZ convertible would be expected to perform differently than estimated, when compared to the 61/39 combination, would be during periods of rising stock prices and

EXHIBIT 2-2
**Convertible price curves for XYZ Company 8 percent, 20-year
convertible bond for different investment values**

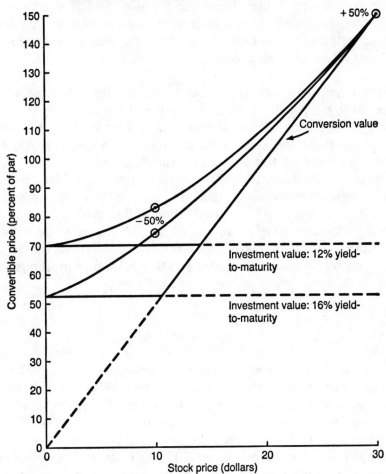

changing interest rates. If interest rates declined while the stock advanced, the combination portfolio would perform better than predicted as unexpected bond gains would be added to stock appreciation. Rising interest rates along with a rising stock price would result in poorer performance for the combination portfolio as bond losses offset stock gains.

The latter event was experienced in recent years as interest rates climbed to historic highs. Despite a bull market in common stocks, those owning combination portfolios faired poorly. As I will show in the next chapter, selected convertibles performed even better than stocks during this period of rising stock prices and they far outpaced stock/straight bond combination portfolios. Many investors, who correctly forecasted the high interest rate market environment, rejected convertible bonds (in favor of common stocks), incorrectly, believing that convertible bonds would suffer as interest rates rose. Those investors missed a lower-risk opportunity that would have appreciated in value more than most higher-risk stock portfolios.

The profit profile

Exhibit 2-3 graphically displays the risk-reward data for XYZ Company securities (Table 2-1), permitting a visual comparison of investment alternatives. The *profit profiles* shown for the convertible bond and common stock illustrate the relative merits of the two securities better than the risk-reward analysis table. As shown, the common stock provides greater profit for a price advance above $21, while the convertible bond offers a higher return (or less risk) at any stock price below $21. A profit profile is a useful portfolio-management tool when comparing alternatives for all possible outcomes.

Many investors would automatically reject the XYZ bond because it is destined to underperform the common at all prices above $21. They might have been sold a good story and "know" that the stock "must" soon rise to $30 or $40 a share. They have probably forgotten that controlling risk is the most important aspect of successful investing. Investors not concerned with risk

EXHIBIT 2-3
Profit profiles for XYZ Company securities (from Table 2-1)

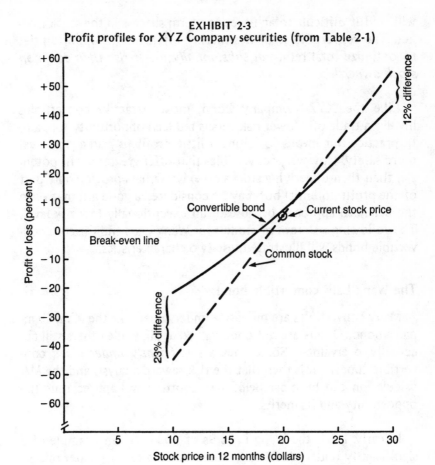

will find it difficult to achieve long-term success in the stock market. The *convertible securities* market offers unique opportunities to optimize total return *at substantially lower risk than common stock ownership.*

Like the XYZ Company bond, most attractive convertibles involve a trade-off—lower risk versus reduced opportunity for gain. In practice this means forfeiting a little profit to gain a great deal more safety. However, convertibles that offer greater profit potential than their underlying stocks do exist. Others provide only part of the profit potential but may be considered a good alternative to the balanced approach because of an exceptionally low risk level. The following risk-reward studies for Wang Labs and Citicorp convertible bonds will illustrate these two characteristics.

The Wang Labs convertible bond

Many convertibles are modestly undervalued like the XYZ Company bond. Others are not undervalued at all, while others still are actually overvalued. Sometimes a *significantly undervalued* convertible appears; it is then that the risk-reward analysis and the MA calculation can be most helpful in spotting and appreciating the opportunity and its merits.

In early 1981, the Wang Labs 9s of 2005 was an example of a significantly undervalued convertible bond offering greater opportunity than its common. Trading at 116 with the Wang Labs common stock at $36, the bond had a conversion premium of only 3 percent while providing a yield advantage of nearly 8 percent. The convertible price curve is shown by Exhibit 2-4 and the risk-reward analysis is presented in Table 2-3.

From the data of Table 2-3, the stock equivalency and market advantage calculations for the bond were:

EXHIBIT 2-4
The convertible price curve for Wang Labs 9s of 2005
convertible bond, January 1981 (conversion ratio = 31.25 shares)

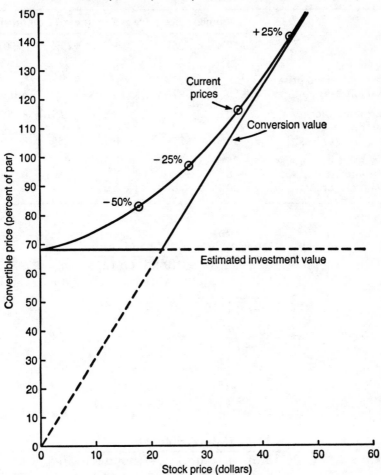

Note: At bond prices above 150, the bond should trade at its conversion value
(stock price multiplied by 31.25).

TABLE 2-3
Risk-reward analysis for Wang Labs 9s of 2005 convertible bond,
January 1981

	Assumed stock price change (next 12 months)				
	−50%	−25%	0%	+25%	+50%
Stock price	18	27	36	45	54
Convertible bond price (Exhibit 2-4)	83	97	116	142	169
Stock gain or loss	−50%	−25%	0%	+ 25%	+ 50%
Plus dividends	0	0	0	0	0
Net profit or loss	−50%	−25%	0%	+ 25%	+ 50%
Convertible gain or loss...	−28%	−16%	0%	+ 22%	+ 46%
Plus interest	+ 8	+ 8	+ 8	+ 8	+ 8
Net profit or loss	−20%	− 8%	+ 8%	+ 30%	+ 54%

$$SE = \frac{(\text{Convertible risk}) - (\text{Bond return})}{(\text{Stock risk}) - (\text{Bond return})}$$

$$= \frac{(-20) - (+14)}{(-50) - (+14)}$$

$$= \frac{-20 - 14}{-50 - 14}$$

$$= \frac{-34}{-64}$$

$$= .53$$

$$MA = \frac{(\text{Convertible return})}{.53(\text{Stock return}) + .47(\text{Bond return})}$$

$$= \frac{+54.0}{.53(+50) + .47(+14)}$$

$$= \frac{+54.0}{+26.5 + 6.6}$$

$$= \frac{+54.0}{+33.1}$$

$$= 1.63$$

Compared directly with its common stock, the bond offered greater opportunity (54 percent versus 50 percent) at less than half the risk (−20 percent versus −50 percent). With a risk level about that of the balanced approach, while providing a much higher profit potential, the Wang Labs convertible was an exceptionally attractive investment opportunity.

Exhibit 2-5 displays the profit profiles for the two securities. It clearly depicts how anyone purchasing the common stock at the time made a serious investment mistake by overlooking an available superior alternative.

One reason that may partially explain why the Wang Labs bond was so undervalued was the possibility of the bond being called for redemption if its price rose to about 130 or higher (Wang had recently called one of its other convertible bond issues). In that event, bondholders would have been forced to convert into common stock, losing both conversion premium (about 1 percent) and up to six months of accrued interest ($45 per bond) in the process. This would have reduced the bond's attractiveness upon a future price advance but not its safety upon a price decline. Assuming the bond would be called in the near future, it nevertheless offered a substantial edge over its common stock (a market advantage of about 1.4).

Since Wang's common stock had a very high beta of 1.75, its convertible bond would be termed an *aggressive* convertible: a possible alternative to good quality common stocks, as indicated in the Introduction. How might the bond be evaluated mathematically as an alternative to the stock market? Let's assume a 20 percent market (having a beta of 1.0) advance or decline over the next year. Allowing an average yield for the market of 5 percent, its total return would be either +25 percent for the advance or −15 percent for the decline. Recognizing that beta numbers include yield, how should the nondividend-paying Wang Labs common stock react to these assumed market changes? Theoretically, the stock should advance by 44 percent (25 percent X 1.75 beta = 44 percent) from $36 to $52, or decline by 26 percent (−15 percent X 1.75 beta = −26 percent) from $36 to $27. From the convertible price curve (Exhibit 2-4), the bond would be expected

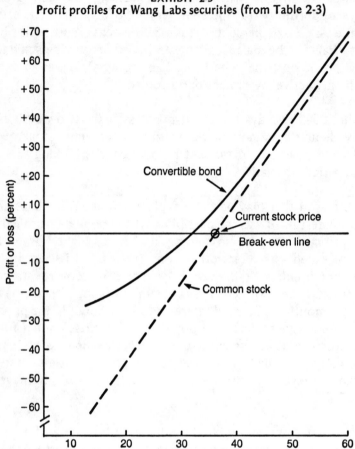

EXHIBIT 2-5
Profit profiles for Wang Labs securities (from Table 2-3)

to trade at 162 for a stock price of $52 and at 97 for a stock price of $27. Including the bond's 8 percent current yield, it would earn a total return of 48 percent on the upside (40 percent gain + 8 percent yield) and lose only 8 percent on the downside (16 percent loss + 8 percent yield).

The Wang Labs convertible bond offered nearly twice the potential of the market at about half the risk.

The investment alternative comparisons in the following table illustrate how undervalued convertibles on high beta stocks can be more attractive than ownership of blue-chip common stocks. Serious investors will usually reject aggressive stocks like Wang Labs, not wishing to incur their high risk. However, convertibles on the same high-risk stocks can often provide more opportunity at less risk than the conservative sector of the market. Convertibles can effectively put high volatility to work in your favor.

Investment alternatives	Total return for a stock market move in one year		
	−20%	0%	+20%
The stock market	−15%	+5%	+25%
Wang Labs common stock	−26	0	+44
Wang Labs convertible bond	− 8	+8	+48

The Citicorp convertible bond

Other significantly undervalued convertibles may offer only a portion of their stock's profit potential at even greater safety. They will usually be trading closer to their investment values and at higher conversion premiums. These convertibles may be viewed as alternatives to the balanced approach.

An example was the Citicorp 5¾s of 2000 bond in early 1981. Trading at 64, with the common at $23, the bond was only 28 percent above its investment value of 50 and had a conversion

value premium of 14 percent. It also provided a 3 percent yield
advantage over its common stock.

Exhibit 2-6 presents the convertible price curve needed to prepare the risk-reward analysis in Table 2-4. Note that a discounted

TABLE 2-4
Risk-reward analysis for Citicorp 5¾s of 2000 convertible bond,
January 1981

	Assumed stock price change (next 12 months)				
	−50%	−25%	0%	+25%	+50%
Stock price	11½	17¼	23	28¾	34½
Estimated bond price					
(Exhibit 2-6)	54	58	65	75	86
Stock gain or loss	−50%	−25%	0%	+25%	+50%
Plus dividends	+ 6	+ 6	+ 6	+ 6	+ 6
Net profit or loss	−44%	−19%	+ 6%	+31%	+56%
Balanced approach gain					
or loss*	−25%	−12%	0%	+12%	+25%
Plus dividends and					
interest*	+10	+10	+10	+10	+10
Net profit or loss	−15%	− 2%	+10%	+22%	+35%
Convertible gain or loss	−16%	− 9%	+ 1%	+17%	+34%
Plus interest	+ 9	+ 9	+ 9	+ 9	+ 9
Net profit or loss	− 7%	0%	+10%	+26%	$43%

*The calculations assume equal dollar investments in Citicorp common yielding 6
percent and straight corporate bonds yielding 14 percent. They also assume that long-
term interest rates remain unchanged over the next 12 months.

bond like Citicorp must rise in value as time passes (and the bond
approaches maturity) even though its common stock's price might
not advance. For this reason, the estimated price curve for the
Citicorp bond was adjusted upward to reflect expected prices 12
months hence (the current bond price is below the curve).

As shown by Table 2-4, the blue-chip Citicorp convertible was
an exceptional alternative to the balanced approach. It offered
greater potential profit (43 percent versus 35 percent) at about
half the risk (−7 percent versus −15 percent). Stock equivalency
and market advantage calculations were:

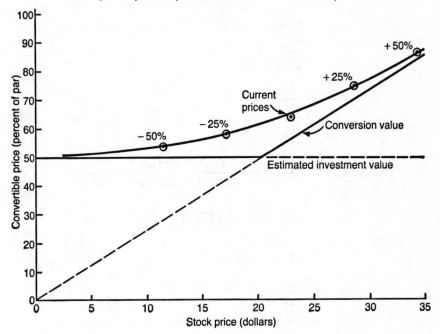

EXHIBIT 2-6
The convertible price curve for Citicorp 5¾s of 2000 convertible bond,
January 1981 (conversion ratio = 24.4 shares)

$$SE = \frac{(Convertible\ risk) - (Bond\ return)}{(Stock\ risk) - (Bond\ return)}$$

$$= \frac{(-7) - (+13)}{(-44) - (+13)}$$

$$= \frac{-7 - 13}{-44 - 13}$$

$$= \frac{-20}{-57}$$

$$= .35$$

$$MA = \frac{(Convertible\ return)}{.35(Stock\ return) + .65(Bond\ return)}$$

$$= \frac{+43.0}{.35(+56) + .65(+13)}$$

$$= \frac{+43.0}{+19.6 + 8.4}$$

$$= \frac{+43.0}{+28.0}$$

$$= 1.54$$

The profit profiles for the two strategies are shown in Exhibit 2-7. As illustrated, low-risk convertibles like Citicorp would be a superior alternative to owning a combination of conservative common stocks and high quality straight bonds.

A unique special situation

An even more striking example of a significantly undervalued convertible bond than Wang Labs or Citicorp was the Louisiana Land Offshore Exploration (LLOE) 5s of 1982. Exchangeable into 80 shares of common stock trading at $12 in the over-the-counter market, the bond's conversion value was 96 (80 shares × $12 per share = $960) and it was available in April 1981 at 98, only 2 points above its conversion value. Since the common paid no dividend, the convertible bond offered greater opportunity than its common stock, similar to Wang Labs. If the common were to

EXHIBIT 2-7
Profit profiles for Citicorp convertible bond and the
balanced approach (from Table 2-4)

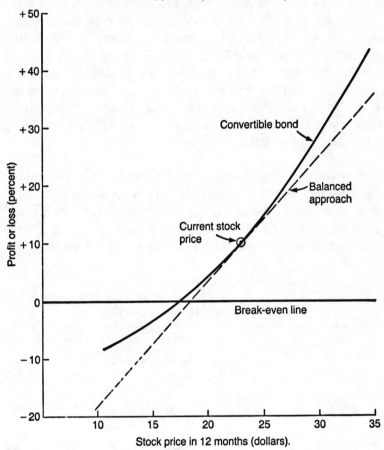

Stock price in 12 months (dollars).

decline, however, there was essentially no risk since the bond could not be worth less than par value when it matured in only one and one half years (October 1, 1982). Perhaps its most unique characteristic was that payment of principal is guaranteed by another, more credit-worthy company, Louisiana Land & Exploration (LLX), a major New York Stock Exchange listed firm. This additional feature is rarely available and illustrates how careful scrutiny can identify unusual opportunities. Convertibles are quite diverse. Note that this particular bond is *not* representative of most convertibles nearing maturity; the market is usually more efficient at assigning fair values.

The risk-reward analysis and profit profiles are presented in Table 2-5 and Exhibit 2-8, assuming the bond was held for the 18 months to maturity. Since the bond offered greater profit than its stock (on any rise in the stock's price) and a 10 percent rate of return regardless of how far the price of the underlying stock

TABLE 2-5
Risk-reward analysis for Louisiana Land Offshore Exploration 5s of 1982 convertible bond, April 1981

	Assumed stock price change (next 18 months)				
	−50%	−25%	0%	+25%	+50%
Stock price	6	9	12	15	18
Convertible bond price . .	100	100	100	120	144
Stock gain or loss	− 50%	− 25%	0%	+ 25%	+ 50%
Plus dividends	0	0	0	0	0
Net profit or loss	− 50%	− 25%	0%	+ 25%	+ 50%
Balanced approach gain or loss*	− 25%	− 12%	0%	+ 12%	+ 25%
Plus dividends and interest	+ 10	+ 10	+ 10	+ 10	+ 10
Net profit or loss	− 15%	− 2%	+ 10%	+ 22%	+ 35%
Convertible gain or loss. . .	+ 2%	+ 2%	+ 2%	+ 22%	+ 47%
Plus interest	+ 8	+ 8	+ 8	+ 8	+ 8
Net profit or loss	+ 10%	+ 10%	+ 10%	+ 30%	+ 55%

*The calculations assume equal dollars in LLOE common and straight corporate bonds yielding 14 percent. They also assume that long-term interest rates remain unchanged over the next 18 months.

EXHIBIT 2-8
Profit profiles for Louisiana Land Offshore Exploration Securities
(from Table 2-5)

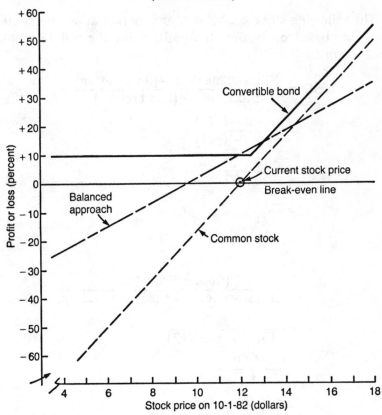

might decline, it was a superior alternative to either its common or to the balanced approach.

The following stock equivalency and market advantage calculations are based on holding the position for the full 18 months until maturity.

$$SE = \frac{(\text{Convertible risk}) - (\text{Bond return})}{(\text{Stock risk}) - (\text{Bond return})}$$

$$= \frac{(+10) - (+21)}{(-50) - (+21)}$$

$$= \frac{+10 - 21}{-50 - 21}$$

$$= \frac{-11}{-71}$$

$$= .15$$

$$MA = \frac{(\text{Convertible return})}{.15(\text{Stock return}) + .85(\text{Bond return})}$$

$$= \frac{+55.0}{.15(+50) + .85(+21)}$$

$$= \frac{+55.0}{7.5 + 17.8}$$

$$= \frac{+55.0}{+25.3}$$

$$= 2.17$$

A market advantage of 2.17 for 18 months was one of the highest I have ever seen. The Louisiana Land Offshore Exploration bond was a truly "heads you win, tails you win" investment opportunity.

Why do undervalued convertibles exist?

Most investors who become aware of undervalued convertibles for the first time are surprised the market allows these opportunities to exist. Their first question is: Why aren't the pros taking advantage of these situations if they are really this attractive? They suspect an error in the risk-reward analysis on the false assumption that the market would never "allow" a security to become that undervalued.

The convertible market is not very efficient, for a number of reasons. First, it takes a high level of expertise and a lot of effort to search out the best opportunities. From over 500 actively traded convertibles, less than 5 percent are significantly under-valued at any given time and the arithmetic is not obvious to the untrained eye.

Next, the convertible market lacks the trading liquidity needed by institutional money managers. When they wish to purchase a few million dollars of a selected stock, they can usually execute their order within a day or two. Except for a handful of the most actively traded convertibles, however, it might take several weeks to accumulate million-dollar-plus convertible positions without disrupting market prices; and there are times it just cannot be done. The only time an institutional-size investor is assured of securing a large convertible position is during the initial offering, at which time the convertible security is not likely to be under-valued.

Finally, brokerage houses seldom recommend convertible bonds or preferreds to their retail clients, who would benefit most from advice of this nature. Brokerage firms either lack the required expertise or believe the low commissions (for convertible bonds) do not justify the extra effort to search out the opportunities, only to have their untrained account executives try to explain them to unsophisticated customers.

Undervalued convertibles do exist and the serious investor should take full advantage of them. This is one of the few areas of the market where small investors can successfully tip the odds in their favor. Convertibles offer such a decisive edge that convertible experts will seldom, if ever, own common stocks or straight bonds. They know there are far better opportunities available in the con-vertible securities market.

CHAPTER 3

Managing a convertible securities portfolio

Conservative investors skilled in the selection of convertible securities seldom buy common stocks or straight bonds. They build their portfolios from carefully chosen convertible bonds and preferreds having attractive risk-reward characteristics.

As illustrated in the last chapter, achieving most of the stock market's potential at substantially less risk is a realistic investment objective with a portfolio of *undervalued* convertibles. This objective can be further refined *to achieve the full potential of the market during good years at no more than half the risk during bad years* by applying the management techniques presented in this chapter.

Building a portfolio

This chapter introduces the tools, guidelines, and selection procedures needed to successfully build and manage your own portfolio of convertible securities. Performance data detailing how these techniques have worked in actual practice will also be covered.

Portfolio diversification

Most individual stock portfolios are inadequately diversified and cannot perform as expected relative to the overall market. Owners of these portfolios are unable to evaluate them against meaningful standards, because they never know whether results are based on luck or their stock selection ability. Other portfolios that attempt "diversification" through a large number of different positions often include stocks in closely related industries and thus defeat the purpose of diversification.

Proper diversification is an essential ingredient for portfolios, which can then be measured against market averages. The bare minimum I recommend is 10 different securities in *unrelated* industries. This, I repeat, is the *absolute minimum* and should be considered only by investors willing to accept the probability that short-term results will depart from the expected performance of larger, well-diversified portfolios.

Bearing in mind the strong likelihood that attractive convertibles may fall within closely related industry groups, I prefer 20 or more different positions and consider broad diversification to be about 40 issues. My experience has shown that highly diversified portfolios display fairly consistent performance. Smaller portfolios are less predictable and usually fluctuate above and below their long-term investment objective. Consequently, small investors often become discouraged after a year or so of below-par performance. Having formed an erroneous conclusion based upon too small a sample of securities and insufficient time, they give up. Believing that convertible investing doesn't work, these investors probably will never return to the convertible arena.

Beta ratings

Since the overall stock market has a beta (volatility) of 1.0, investors should pay attention to beta ratings for the underlying common stocks of their convertible selections. If the objective is to match the market during upward moves, the common stocks should have an average beta of about 1.2. This above-average profit potential will compensate for the fact that most convertibles trail their stocks during price advances (e.g., the XYZ Company bond of Chapter 2). If you are willing to accept about three fourths of a market advance, the underlying stocks may have an average beta of about .9. Note that the downside risk for convertibles will be less than stock betas would suggest because of the convertibles' characteristic price curves.

Beta ratings may be obtained from a number of different sources including *The Value Line Investment Survey*[1] (published weekly) and Merrill Lynch's bimonthly *Quantitative Analysis*.[2] Notice, however, that beta calculations are not uniform among the services. For example, both employ a five-year time frame but *Value Line* computes betas relative to the New York Stock Exchange Index and Merrill Lynch uses the Standard & Poor's 500. (There are additional differences between their specific formulas.)

---

[1] Available from Arnold Bernhard & Co., 711 Third Avenue, New York, N.Y. 10017 (covers 1,650 stocks).

[2] Available from Merrill Lynch stockbrokers (covers about 900 stocks).

Since any beta is a measurement of past price action, all beta figures should be treated as educated guesses about what might happen in the future. While any single beta could fail completely in forecasting future price movements, I believe the average beta for a diversified portfolio to be a useful figure.

Fundamental and technical analysis

Proponents of the efficient market concept advise that neither fundamental nor technical analysis of common stocks will help investors outguess the market. Their proclamations are based on computer studies of historical price data at prestigious universities. In essence they are advocating a buy-and-hold strategy. Most money managers and stockbrokers disagree with their conclusions for various reasons (e.g., management fees and brokerage commissions earned from active portfolio management).

Without taking a firm stand in favor of the efficient market, I must advise that successful investing in convertibles is more consistent with the efficient market approach. I am not suggesting that you throw darts at the financial pages to pick your securities, as some efficient market proponents would. I am suggesting that your time will be better spent in searching out the handful of outstanding convertibles that are inefficiently priced than in studying common stocks. Those who pick stocks first, then check to see if there is an attractive convertible as an alternative, might as well forget about a convertible securities program. The chances of finding significantly undervalued convertibles on stocks they have chosen are slim; and it is almost certain they will miss the special situations (e.g., the Louisiana Land Offshore Exploration bond of Chapter 2).

My own approach is to first select the best possible convertible candidates without regard for the underlying stocks. Then as a final step in the decision process, I evaluate the stocks based on fundamental and technical factors. Usually about 20 percent of the tentative convertible candidates are rejected as a result of this final review.

Research

The key to successful investing in convertible securities is research: a systematic and careful evaluation of all possible candidates to uncover the few that offer exceptional risk-reward characteristics. Other tools discussed in this chapter are important but not nearly as crucial as finding the best opportunities.

A convenient source of statistical data that includes conversion ratios and investment values is an absolute must. There are several brokerage firms and advisory services that provide some of this data. The best is *Value Line Convertibles,* published weekly.[3] This service is used by almost all convertible specialists. *Value Line* includes not only investment values, risk-reward estimates, and other important statistical data but in-depth information on specific securities via footnotes, special bulletins, and individual company studies.

Guidelines for buying convertibles

The following basic guidelines are the result of years of study and my personal experience in varying markets. They should not be taken lightly since they virtually assure your consistently outperforming the market.

1. Determine your investment objective relative to the stock market as measured by a meaningful index, such as the Standard & Poor's 500. Do you want to fully participate in an advancing market at about half the risk if the market were to decline? Are you willing to give up some of the opportunity to attain even greater safety? These are important decisions because they will govern your selection of convertibles to buy, and will also provide you with a means to measure your progress.
2. Decide how much diversification you want. I would suggest a minimum of 20 issues in diverse industries, with approximately equal dollars invested in each position. If you find two attractive situations in the same industry group, consider taking

---

[3] Available from Arnold Bernhard & Co., 711 Third Avenue, New York, N.Y. 10017.

smaller positions in each. Should you find more than 20 different candidates, don't hesitate to increase the total number of positions. (Bear in mind that broad diversification will require you to monitor a larger number of securities.)

3. Establish disciplined procedures for evaluating potential candidates and always prepare a risk-reward analysis. If you desire the full potential of the market, search for undervalued convertibles trading close to conversion value (but not too far above their investment floors). The underlying stocks should have above-average price volatility on average. Another option is to balance the portfolio by including convertibles where the underlying stock has below-average volatility and those having higher volatility. I recommend the latter approach: it broadens your choice. It also assures more consistent performance since the market prefers low-volatility, blue-chip stocks at certain times and secondary issues at other times.

4. Purchase convertibles on stocks with which you are comfortable. You may apply your own fundamental or technical analysis to the underlying common stocks, or rely, as I do, on an investment advisory service that is better equipped for the task. Remember, however, this is the *last* step in the selection process. The best convertible candidates should be chosen first.

Specific selection procedures

Assuming you desire a convertible securities portfolio that can match the Standard & Poor's 500 stock index at about half the risk, here are the specific selection procedures.

1. *Upside potential.* Select only convertibles that will advance at least 30 percent for a 50 percent stock advance (excluding interest or dividends). The overall portfolio should average about 40 percent.

2. *Underlying stock risk.* The stocks underlying the convertibles should have an average beta of about 1.2. This above-average stock volatility is necessary to compensate for conversion premium loss during a market advance.

3. *Downside risk.* Any convertible selected should be expected to decline not more than 30 percent for a 50 percent move by

its underlying common, and the portfolio should average
under 25 percent. Thus the risk level of the total portfolio will
be about that of the balanced approach of common stocks and
straight bonds.
4. *Yield advantage.* The portfolio of convertibles should usually
   provide a current yield advantage of about 2 percent over the
   underlying common stocks.
5. *Market advantage.* Including yields for both the common and
   convertible securities, each convertible should offer a market
   advantage of at least 1.25, and the overall portfolio should
   average about 1.4.

Undervalued convertible bonds available
in August 1981

Table 3-1 presents a list of 20 undervalued convertible bonds
having common stocks listed on the New York Stock Exchange.
Prices were representative of actual market conditions at the time,
and price projections were determined by the author. Each convertible offered a market advantage of more than 1.25, as displayed in the right-hand column of Table 3-1.

Convertibles were included solely because of their favorable
market advantages: No consideration was given to fundamental or
technical factors relating to their underlying stocks or to diversification among different industry groups. Although the list of convertibles was a preliminary screen, subject to further refinement,
we can today draw important conclusions about the availability of
undervalued candidates at the time.

1. *Upside potential.* For a 50 percent stock advance, the convertibles were expected to advance 39 percent, on average. This
   compared favorably with our objective of 40 percent.
2. *Underlying stock risk.* Stock betas ranged from .85 (Grey-
   hound and Ralston Purina) up to 1.75 (Hutton Group). The
   average was 1.20—right in line with our objective. Note that it
   was not necessary to consider lower-quality bonds trading on
   the American Stock Exchange to reach our above-average beta
   target.

TABLE 3-1
Undervalued convertible bonds listed on the New York Stock Exchange, August 1981

Company	Convertible description	Convertible price	Current yield		Leverage*		Beta†	SE‡	MA§
			Stock	Convertible	-50%	+50%			
Allied Corp. (Textron)	7.75-05	93	4.8%	8.3%	-22%	+37%	1.20	38%	1.58
Anheuser Busch	9.00-05	108	3.1	8.3	-23	+35	0.90	46	1.39
Bally Manufacturing	6.00-98	86	0.4	7.0	-25	+33	1.35	50	1.25
Becton Dickinson	5.00-89	75	2.3	6.7	-17	+32	0.80	38	1.41
Chase Manhattan	6.50-96	88	6.2	7.4	-30	+48	1.00	64	1.36
Citicorp	5.75-00	72	5.3	5.9	-24	+50	1.15	54	1.57
Dean Witter Reynolds	10.00-05	114	2.7	8.8	-27	+45	1.55	52	1.58
Georgia Pacific	5.25-96	80	5.2	6.6	-24	+40	1.05	52	1.33
Greyhound	6.50-90	88	7.5	7.4	-24	+49	0.85	54	1.47
Hercules	6.50-99	70	6.0	9.3	-17	+35	1.20	36	1.54
Hospital Corp, America	8.75-06	106	0.9	8.2	-22	+32	1.25	43	1.38
Hutton (E.F.) Group	9.50-05	110	2.3	8.6	-24	+39	1.75	48	1.47
Inexco Oil	8.50-00	120	0.4	7.1	-32	+48	1.35	62	1.53
Kaiser Cement	9.00-05	90	5.6	10.0	-17	+30	1.00	36	1.40
Merrill Lynch	9.25-05	101	3.7	9.2	-18	+31	1.55	36	1.48
Ralston Purina	5.75-00	79	6.3	7.3	-25	+42	0.85	54	1.38
Security Pacific	9.75-06	99	6.1	9.8	-15	+35	1.20	31	1.72
Signal Cos. (Ampex)	5.50-94	82	2.8	6.7	-25	+37	1.30	52	1.28
Storage Technology	10.25-00	122	0	8.4	-28	+46	1.50	53	1.66
U.S. Air	8.25-05	94	0.8	8.8	-23	+31	1.20	44	1.28
Averages			3.6%	8.0%	-23%	+39%	1.20	47%	1.45

*The projected percent change for the convertible for changes in the price of the underlying stock of −50 percent or +50 percent.

† *Value Line* betas.

‡Stock equivalency (SE) describes an alternative investment in common stock and straight bonds. The figure shown is the percent invested in stock (e.g., 45 percent means 45 percent stock and 55 percent straight bonds).

§The market advantage (MA) indicates whether the convertible is undervalued (above 1.0) or overvalued (below 1.0) for stock price changes of −50 percent or +50 percent over a 12-month period. Based on investment values estimated by *Value Line Convertibles*.

3. *Downside risk.* The average potential loss of 23 percent for the portfolio was below our target of half the market risk for a downward move of 50 percent. Considering a portfolio beta of 1.2, the overall risk level was about the same as for the balanced approach.
4. *Yield advantage.* The 3.6 percent average yield for the underlying common stocks was somewhat below that of the popular market indexes like the Standard & Poor's 500. This below-average yield would be expected for a portfolio of higher beta stocks. The 8 percent average for the convertible portfolio provided an exceptionally high yield advantage of 4.4 percent, compared to our 2 percent objective. This reflects the very high interest rates prevailing at the time.
5. *Stock equivalency.* Although a specific SE parameter was not included in the selection procedures, it is inherent in the downside risk objective near that of the balanced approach. This is confirmed by the average stock equivalency of 47 percent from Table 3-1.
6. *Market advantage.* The average MA of 1.45 for the 20 issues is confirmed by a single calculation for the overall portfolio.

$$MA = \frac{\text{(Convertible return)}}{.47\text{(Stock return)} + .53\text{(Bond return)}}$$

$$= \frac{(+39.0 + 8.0)}{.47(+50.0 + 3.6) + .53(+13.5)}$$

$$= \frac{+47.0}{+25.2 + 7.2}$$

$$= \frac{+47.0}{+32.4}$$

$$= 1.45$$

Convertible bonds offered phenomenal alternatives to the stock market in August 1981.

Guidelines for selling convertibles

Since convertibles are selected on the basis of common sense and mathematical relationships, portfolios should be monitored

along the same lines. I recommend four basic guidelines for decid-
ing when to sell. When any one of the following conditions are
met, the convertible should be sold and replaced with a new selection that meets the original criteria.

1. *The convertible's price advances.* As the underlying common
   stock advances and the convertible loses its market advantage
   by moving well above its investment floor, take profits. The
   convertible will no longer provide the downside safety that is
   sought. By replacing that convertible with a new one, you
   realize a profit and you also protect the profit by again buying
   convertibles that meet the original selection guidelines.
2. *The convertible's price declines.* When the common stock
   declines, the convertible will lag behind as it approaches its
   investment value. The convertible has fulfilled its function of
   protecting you. It has decreased less than the common and
   now takes on more of the characteristics of a straight debt
   instrument. Because the conversion premium has increased,
   the convertible will now trail well behind its stock on any
   future price advance. If the convertible will not move up at
   least 20 percent for a 50 percent stock advance, it should be
   sold.
3. *The convertible loses its undervaluation.* Any time a convertible loses its favorable risk-reward characteristics, it should be
   sold. We are working in an area where inefficiencies often
   develop. For no apparent reason you may find the common
   going down and the convertible going up, or the convertible
   declining by less than was expected. In either case, a new MA
   calculation may indicate that the convertible is no longer
   undervalued. Take advantage of these market inefficiencies by
   replacing that convertible with a superior alternative.
4. *A marginal convertible may be sold to take advantage of an
   exceptional alternative.* Since you should continually keep
   your portfolio in positions that will participate in a market
   advance at low risk, a marginal convertible—one that has not
   quite reached a point where a sell is indicated—may be replaced
   with an exceptional alternative.

These basic guidelines provide a systematic framework for continually monitoring your portfolio. They will allow you to main-

tain the most advantageous risk-reward posture for participation in an advancing market and for protection in a declining market. You will never become "married" to any security you own. It is one of the few sure ways I have ever seen that allows you to remove any emotion from investing while increasing the odds in your favor.

Executing orders for buying or selling convertibles

The next guidelines should be carefully followed when placing buy or sell orders:

1. Select convertibles that are actively traded whenever possible— they will normally be listed on the New York Stock Exchange and have a large issue size outstanding.
2. Monitor both the convertible and its underlying stock prices prior to entering orders—a good "feel" for their related prices will save you money, whether buying or selling, by permitting you to execute orders at favorable prices. (Give this monitoring responsibility to a stockbroker, who is better equipped for the job.)
3. Place orders through a brokerage firm that has skills in executing listed bond orders in the over-the-counter (off-board) market—many listed bonds are more actively traded off-the-board than on the floor of an exchange.
4. Work with a stockbroker who has special training in evaluating convertibles and in executing orders—the broker's knowledge and skills are much more critical to your investment success in this area than in buying or selling common stocks or straight bonds.

Actual investment experience

I first become interested in convertible securities as a private investor during the go-go days of the 1960s. In 1971, I joined the brokerage community as a stockbroker and began recommending positions to clients. By 1975, I had started managing accounts that employed convertible bonds and preferreds as part of a number of convertible strategies in their management. These strategies included convertibles ranging from the aggressive sector of the market (e.g., Wang Labs) to the very blue-chip area (e.g., Citicorp).

Appendixes B and C to this chapter present all listed convertible bonds and preferreds employed by the largest account (determined quarterly) under my full management over the six-year period from 1976 through 1981. For evaluation purposes, I separated the convertibles into two groups. Appendix B lists convertibles whose underlying common stocks were ranked below B+ by Standard & Poor's; Appendix C lists convertibles of higher quality stocks (including high-quality financial stocks, which are never ranked by this rating service).

The convertibles of Appendix B generally may be considered *aggressive* and those of Appendix C *low-risk.* Although a detailed risk-reward analysis for each convertible and a beta figure for its common stock would be necessary to precisely describe each convertible, I believe these two categories to be sufficiently discriminating for meaningful comparisons. The tables cover 265 different positions, broken down as follows:

	Number of bonds	Number of preferreds	Total number
Aggressive	83	12	95
Low-risk	103	67	170
Totals	186	79	265

Both appendixes display the month each convertible was purchased and sold, the number of months held, and the net total return for each position. All interest or dividends received, capital gain or loss, and brokerage commissions are included.

Analysis of performance

Appendix D provides a quarterly performance analysis over the same six-year period. Since the number of issues employed varied from quarter to quarter, I assumed equal dollar investments would have been made in each security, and also assumed portfolio adjustments for equal dollars at the end of each quarter. To this extent, resulting performance data must be considered hypothetical. Buy and sell prices are factual and brokerage commissions are included.

Table 3-2 compares the two convertible portfolios with the Standard & Poor's 500 index and the balanced approach. Aggressive convertibles outperformed the S&P 500 every year except 1980 (a virtual tie). For the entire six-year period, the aggressive convertible group gained 257 percent, versus 83 percent for the S&P 500. The low-risk convertible group beat the balanced approach every year and ended the six-year period ahead by 181 percent, versus 45 percent—four times better.

Exhibits 3-1 and 3-2 graphically compare the aggressive and low-risk convertible portfolios with the S&P 500 and the balanced approach, respectively.

I expect some readers to challenge these performance results on the basis that 265 positions over six years do not represent a sufficiently large sample. I cannot disagree. I would like to gain additional experience with more issues and a longer time frame before drawing hard conclusions. However, the four publicly traded (closed-end) convertible funds also demonstrated superior performance during this same period—thus my experience is not an isolated test of the merits of convertible securities.[4]

I also believe the results are conservative when considering the portfolio management guidelines presented in this chapter. For instance, a convertible offering modest risk-reward advantages might have been purchased as part of a hedging strategy (to be presented in a later chapter) because of the availability of an attractive call option. The convertible might also have been sold prematurely when the option expired or held longer than normal while awaiting the option's expiration date.

For these reasons, I believe past results understate profit potential when relating them to a portfolio of significantly undervalued

---

[4] The four publicly traded convertible funds are American General Convertible Securities and Chase Convertible Fund on the New York Stock Exchange and Bancroft Convertible Fund and Castle Convertible Fund on the American Stock Exchange.

TABLE 3-2
Comparison of convertibles purchased with appropriate market indexes

Year	S&P 500 stock index*	Salomon Brothers bond index*	Balanced approach†	Low-risk convertibles‡	Aggressive convertibles‡
1976	+23.8%	+18.6%	+21.2%	+38.6%	+33.1%
1977	− 7.2	+ 1.7	− 2.8	+ 4.8	+ 9.0
1978	+ 6.6	− 0.1	+ 3.3	+10.9	+30.4
1979	+18.4	− 4.2	+ 7.1	+19.9	+36.8
1980	+32.5	− 2.6	+15.0	+29.1	+32.1
1981	− 5.0	− 1.0	− 3.0	+12.7	+ 4.4
6-year cumulative return	+82.6%	+11.4%	+45.4%	+181.0%	+256.9%
Annual compounded return	+10.6%	+ 1.8%	+ 6.4%	+ 18.8%	+ 23.6%

*The Standard & Poor's 500 stock index and Salomon Brothers bond index both assume that dividends or bond interest are reinvested and *exclude* security handling expenses, order execution costs, and management fees.
†The balanced approach is based on funds being equally split between stocks and bonds.
‡Net return including expenses for order execution and account management.

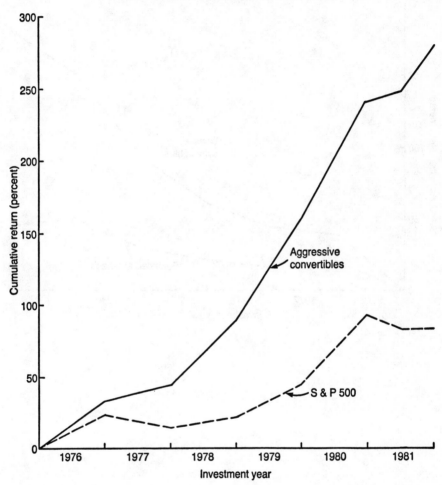

EXHIBIT 3-1
Six-year cumulative returns: Aggressive convertibles versus
Standard & Poor's 500 (from Table 3-2)

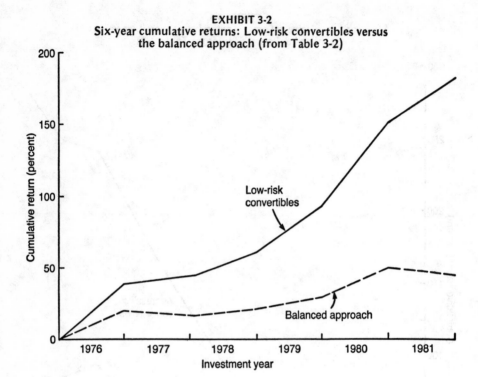

EXHIBIT 3-2
Six-year cumulative returns: Low-risk convertibles versus
the balanced approach (from Table 3-2)

convertibles purchased and sold on their own merits. In addition, the buy and sell guidelines have been continuously refined to reflect my experience under a variety of market conditions. Therefore, the future should offer even greater opportunity.

Appendixes B and C also document 42 realized losses among the 219 convertibles closed. This may seem to be a high number of losers, considering that cash flow (interest or dividends) is included in the calculations and that the overall stock market was in a long-term uptrend during the entire period. In retrospect, most of the losers would have become profitable had they been held longer. In comparison to strategies where investors seldom take losses, however, one of the main keys to successful convertible investing is the replacement of positions that have lost their favorable risk-reward characteristics (whether profitable or not) with available, more attractive candidates.

Although selected convertibles are, by themselves, inherently safer than conventional stocks and bonds, there are ways to remove virtually all risks from a convertible securities investment program. The next two chapters will present convertible hedging strategies employing common stock and listed options. These strategies are presently being used by conservative investors desiring superior alternatives to money market instruments or straight bonds—corporates *and* tax-exempts.

APPENDIX B

Convertibles on stocks rated
below B+ by Standard & Poor's
employed during the six-year
study, 1976 through 1981

Company	Convertible description	Purchase data		Sale data		Months held	Net total return
		Date	Price	Date	Price		
Pan American	7.50 -98	12-75	78.00	6-76	92.75	6	+ 21%
Occidental Petroleum	$ 3.60 pfd.	12-75	46.88	6-76	57.25	6	+ 22
El Paso	6.00 -93	3-76	83.00	1-77	93.00	10	+ 16
Avco	9.625-01	10-76	103.50	12-76	106.00	2	+ 2
Pan American	7.50 -98	10-76	76.25	3-77	76.88	5	+ 2
Riegel Textile	5.00 -93	12-76	77.50	6-78	80.00	18	+ 10
Budd Company	5.875-94	12-76	91.88	1-78	142.00	13	+ 59
Wallace Murray	6.50 -91	12-76	100.00	3-77	118.00	3	+ 18
Grumman	4.25 -92	1-77	61.50	6-77	69.75	5	+ 13
Oak Industries	4.375-87	5-77	70.00	6-77	72.00	1	+ 1
Avco	9.625-01	6-77	114.50	7-78	160.50	13	+ 47
Pan American	7.50 -98	6-77	88.50	9-78	120.00	15	+ 43
Arvin Industries	$ 2.00 pfd.	6-77	28.00	5-78	33.40	9	+ 21
Curtiss Wright	$ 2.00 pfd.	6-77	27.25	10-77	26.00	4	— 6
Grumman	8.00 -99	7-77	111.00	5-78	109.25	10	+ 3
National City Lines	5.50 -88	10-77	70.00	7-78	60.00	9	— 11
Republic N.Y.	5.375-97	11-77	74.50	7-78	91.00	8	+ 24
Cooper Laboratories	4.50 -92	12-77	66.50	9-79a	63.50	21	+ 4
Kaiser Cement	$ 2.50 pfd.	1-78	34.62	8-78	50.00	7	+ 43
Western Airlines	5.25 -93	4-78	80.00	6-78	104.00	2	+ 28
Allegheny Airlines	9.25 -99	5-78	131.00	6-78	182.00	1	+ 38
Phoenix Steel	6.00 -87	6-78	84.00	3-79	70.00	9	— 14
TRE Corp.	9.75 -02	6-78	124.88	9-78	126.00	3	+ 1
General Instrument	10.25 -96	6-78	124.50	8-78	132.75	2	+ 6
Eastern Airlines	10.00 -02	6-78	123.50	8-78	137.00	2	+ 11
Mohawk Data Sciences	12.00 -89	7-78	126.00	9-78	124.00	2	— 2

Company	Convertible description	Purchase data		Sale data		Months held	Net total return
		Date	Price	Date	Price		
Litton Industries	3.50 -87	8-78	70.00	6-80b	115.00	22	+ 70%
Ramada Inns	10.00 -00	8-78	126.00	9-78	159.00	1	+ 25
Kaiser Cement	$ 1.375 pfd.	8-78	19.50	8-79	22.50	12	+ 18
McDonnell Douglas	4.75 -91	9-78	118.00	1-79	114.00	4	− 4
Pan American	9.875-96	10-78	117.00	12-78	122.50	2	+ 4
Western Airlines	5.25 -93	11-78	84.00	7-79	95.00	8	+ 15
Ramada Inns	10.00 -00	11-78	117.00	5-79	173.50	6	+ 50
Di Giorgio	5.75 -93	11-78	74.50	1-79	82.00	2	+ 9
El Paso	6.00 -93	12-78	90.25	2-79	102.00	2	+ 12
LTV Corp.	$ 2.60 pfd.	1-79	24.38	6-80	29.50	17	+ 31
Punta Gorda Isles	$ 1.104 pfd.	4-79	11.75	9-79a	12.88	5	+ 9
Texasgulf	$ 3.00 pfd.	5-79	41.50	10-79	50.25	4	+ 20
Conn. General Mortgage	6.00 -96	8-79	81.00	10-80	93.00	14	+ 21
Grumman	8.00 -99	9-79	102.00	1-80	142.00	4	+ 39
NFC Corp.	8.00 -92	9-79b	93.50	11-80	122.75	14	+ 39
Trans World	5.00 -94	9-79b	58.00	5-80	44.00	8	− 22
UAL Corp.	4.25 -92	10-79	55.00	10-81	40.00	24	− 15
Western Airlines	5.25 -93	11-79	75.00	12-79	93.00	1	+ 22
Sherwin Williams	6.25 -95	12-79	71.00	5-80	73.00	5	+ 4
Fairmont Foods	9.00 -96	12-79	94.62	6-80	106.00	6	+ 14
Phoenix Steel	6.00 -87	2-80	65.00	5-80	65.00	3	− 1
National Kinney	5.25 -97	2-80	44.00	7-80	39.38	5	− 10
Sanders Associates	7.00 -92	3-80	76.50	5-80	82.50	2	+ 7
Mattel	$ 2.50 pfd.	3-80	20.00	5-80	23.25	2	+ 15

Company	Coupon	Mat.	Date 1	Price 1	Date 2	Price 2	No.	Chg.
Ramada Inns	10.00	-00	4-80	109.50	6-81	141.90	14	+ 38
Ozark Air Lines	5.25	-86	5-80	64.75	4-81	130.64	11	+104
LTV Corp.	12.00	-05	6-80	101.50	2-81	198.35	8	+100
Cooper Laboratories	4.50	-92	6-80c	64.75	12-80	84.60	6	+ 7
Warnaco	$ 1.50	pfd.	6-80c	29.25	3-81	36.55	9	+ 25
Grumman	11.00	-00	7-80	117.00	open			
Allegheny Ludlum	4.00	-81	7-80	95.80	7-80	100.00	1	+ 3
American Airlines	5.25	-98	10-80	48.94	2-81	55.50	4	+ 13
Zenith Radio	8.375	-05	10-80	102.00	open			
Energy Resources	9.00	-95	10-80	103.80	open			
U.S. Realty Investment	5.75	-89	11-80	75.82	4-81	88.48	5	+ 17
Ampex	5.50	-94	11-80	77.50	12-80	84.50	1	+ 10
Western Union	$ 4.60	pfd.	11-80	56.25	10-81	58.04	9	+ 4
Inexco Oil	8.50	-00	12-80	119.50	open			
Crystal Oil	11.375	-00	1-81	112.58	3-81	150.00	2	+ 33
Computer Sciences	6.00	-94	1-81	83.00	open			
Prime Computer	10.00	-00	1-81	130.00	3-81	112.50	2	— 14
Macrodyne	12.50	-95	1-81	108.00	open			
Newbery Energy	12.00	-95	2-81	87.00	open			
Columbia Pictures	8.25	-00	2-81	104.00	open			
Vishay Intertechnology	11.00	-00	2-81	88.00	open			
Instrument Systems	12.00	-99	3-81	94.25	8-81	79.50	5	— 12
Eastern Airlines	11.75	-05	4-81	96.62	open			
Recognition Equipment	11.00	-06	4-81	115.00	open			
Transtechnology	12.50	-01	4-81	98.00	open			
GAF Corp.	$ 1.20	pfd.	4-81	15.75	6-81	18.94	2	+ 17
MGM Grand Hotels	9.50	-00	4-81	79.23	open			
Energy Management	12.00	-96	5-81	104.00	open			
Sanders Associates	7.00	-92	5-81	107.00	open			
Health Chem	10.375	-99	5-81	102.75	open			

APPENDIX B *(concluded)*

Company	Convertible description	Purchase data		Sale data		Months held	Net total return
		Date	Price	Date	Price		
TIE Communications	11.50 -01	5-81	114.00	open			
Punta Gorda Isles	6.00 -92	6-81	73.50	open			
Fuqua Industries	5.75 -88	6-81	75.00	open			
Trans World	12.00 -05	6-81	113.00	11-81	96.00	5	− 12%
Prime Computer	10.00 -05	6-81	124.00	11-81	103.00	5	− 15
PSA Inc.	11.125-04	7-81	108.50	open			
Ramada Inns	10.00 -00	7-81	108.50	open			
Nat'l. Education	9.875-00	7-81	103.62	open			
Tacoma Boatbuilding	10.75 -01	8-81	95.50	open			
Fairfield Communities	9.75 -03	8-81	107.08	open			
Crystal Oil	11.375-00	9-81	104.50	open			
Galaxy Oil	9.00 -94	10-81	100.00	open			
Brunswick	10.00 -06	10-81	99.00	open			
Pogo Producing	8.00 -05	10-81	82.00	open			
Four-Phase Systems	9.125-01	12-81	91.12	open			

Note: This table presents aggressive convertibles purchased for the author's largest managed accounts beginning late 1975. The term *aggressive* is defined as convertibles whose underlying common stocks were rated lower than B+ by Standard & Poor's. Over-the-counter securities were excluded since they usually lack trading liquidity. The net total return figures include interest received, capital gain or loss, and roundtrip commissions. Where an account was replaced by a new larger account, end of the quarter prices were used to close out an older convertible not held by the new account or to establish starting prices for convertibles held by the new account not held by the former. These are shown by a, b, or c for the three clients involved in the study.

APPENDIX C

Convertibles on stocks rated B+
or higher by Standard & Poor's
and high-quality financial
stocks employed during the
six-year study, 1976 through
1981

Company	Convertible description	Purchase data		Sale data		Months held	Net total return
		Date	Price	Date	Price		
Chase Manhattan	4.875-93	12-75	61.00	4-76	68.25	4	+11%
Federal Nat'l Mtg.	4.375-96	12-75	77.75	1-76	82.00	1	+ 3
Gulf & Western	5.50 -93	12-75	82.00	1-76	95.50	1	+14
Tesoro Petroleum	5.25 -89	12-75	82.75	1-77	102.00	13	+27
United Technologies	4.50 -92	12-75	66.50	4-76	88.25	4	+32
International Tel. & Tel.	$ 2.25 pfd.	12-75	41.00	1-76	45.00	1	+ 6
Greyhound	6.50 -90	1-76	82.25	8-76	90.75	7	+12
Grace	6.50 -96	5-76	94.12	12-76	99.50	7	+ 8
Federal Nat'l Mtg.	4.375-96	5-76	72.75	10-76	80.75	5	+11
International Tel. & Tel.	$ 2.25 pfd.	6-76	31.25	8-76	38.62	2	+21
Woolworth	$ 2.20 pfd.	7-76	35.00	12-76	37.50	5	+ 6
Ford Motor	4.875-98	8-76	82.50	8-78	85.38	24	+13
Gulf & Western	5.50 -93	10-76	90.75	4-77	78.25	6	−13
National Distillers	4.50 -92	12-76	95.00	11-77	87.25	9	− 7
American Hoist	5.50 -93	12-76	89.00	5-77	123.00	5	+38
Continental Telephone	5.25 -86	12-76	82.50	9-77	85.25	9	+ 6
Beech Aircraft	4.75 -93	12-76	81.00	12-77	96.00	12	+22
Airco	3.875-87	12-76	96.00	6-77	105.00	6	+ 9
U.V. Industries	5.75 -93	12-76	81.25	8-78	94.71	20	+26
North Amer. Philips	4.00 -92	12-76	77.44	6-77	77.39	6	0
Hilton Hotels	5.50 -95	12-76	85.50	6-77	87.00	6	+ 3
Parker Hannifan	4.00 -92	12-76	74.62	6-77	87.00	6	+16
Storer Broadcasting	4.50 -86	12-76	85.00	5-77	86.12	5	+ 1
Federal Nat'l Mtg.	4.375-96	12-76	85.75	8-78	99.00	20	+21
GAF Corp.	$ 1.20 pfd.	12-76	18.58	2-77	18.69	8	+ 2
White Consolidated	5.50 -93	1-77	101.50	6-77	106.50	5	+ 5

Company							
City Investing	7.50 -90	1-77	99.50	6-77	104.75	5	+ 6
Zapata	4.75 -88	2-77	70.91	7-77	70.94	5	0
Houston Industries	5.50 -85	2-77	94.50	10-80	80.50	44	+ 4
Citicorp	5.75 -00	2-77	94.50	3-78	75.12	13	−16
E-Systems	4.50 -92	2-77	86.25	11-77	84.00	9	− 1
Melville	4.875-96	2-77	89.00	4-78	94.00	14	+10
Tesoro Petroleum	5.25 -89	2-77	94.00	9-77	80.00	7	−14
Ogden	5.00 -93	3-77	71.00	1-78	69.00	10	0
Sola Basic	4.50 -92	3-77	90.12	5-77	120.00	2	+31
Woolworth	$ 2.20 pfd.	4-77	34.50	11-77	30.00	7	−13
Dayco	6.25 -96	5-77	93.00	7-79	100.00	26	+20
Castle & Cooke	5.375-94	5-77	79.00	8-78	110.50	15	+45
Harrah's	7.50 -96	6-77	111.50	5-78	147.00	11	+36
Lear Siegler	$ 2.25 pfd.	6-77	41.00	2-78	37.75	8	− 7
Texasgulf Inc.	$ 3.00 pfd.	10-77	39.50	5-78	38.50	7	− 2
Hilton Hotels	5.50 -95	11-77	86.75	5-78	115.00	6	+33
Pennwalt	$ 1.60 pfd.	11-77	23.50	7-78	24.38	8	+ 5
Foremost McKesson	$ 1.80 pfd.	11-77	28.83	5-78	34.25	6	+18
Amerada Hess	$ 3.50 pfd.	12-77	62.88	4-78	64.00	4	0
Gulf & Western	$ 2.50 pfd.	12-77	30.25	5-78	34.00	5	+12
Beech Aircraft	4.75 -93	1-78	91.00	2-78	102.00	1	+10
Chromalloy American	$ 5.00 pfd.	1-78	63.00	6-78	92.79	5	+48
Carrier	$ 1.86 pfd.	2-78	27.75	4-78	34.50	2	+21
Holiday Inns	$ 1.70 pfd.	2-78	24.50	4-78	26.22	2	+ 3
Humana	6.00 -99	4-78	100.00	7-78	122.72	3	+22
Textron	$ 1.40 pfd.	4-78	23.50	6-78	26.66	2	+10
GAF Corp.	$ 1.20 pfd.	4-78	16.42	9-80	17.50	29	+21
McDermott	$ 2.20 pfd.	4-78	31.88	9-78	33.00	5	+ 3
White Consolidated	5.50 -92	5-78	90.50	6-78	91.00	1	− 1
Gulf & Western	5.50 -93	5-78	84.50	2-80	105.00	21	+33

APPENDIX C *(continued)*

Company	Convertible description	Purchase data		Sale data		Months held	Net total return
		Date	Price	Date	Price		
City Investing	7.50 -90	5-78	101.25	7-79	111.50	14	+17%
Wometco Enterprises	5.50 -94	6-78	96.00	8-78	111.00	2	+14
Household Finance	$ 2.50 pfd.	6-78	32.50	6-80b	28.50	24	− 1
Zale	$ 0.80 pfd.	6-78	13.38	8-78	14.38	2	+ 3
Storer Broadcasting	4.50 -86	7-78	90.55	4-79	111.50	9	+24
Fruehauf	5.50 -94	7-78	76.50	6-79	83.00	11	+12
Lone Star Industries	5.125-93	7-78	85.00	6-79	95.00	11	+15
Carrier	$ 1.86 pfd.	7-78	33.75	12-78	50.21	5	+47
Rockwell International	4.25 -91	8-78	78.48	3-79	80.75	7	+ 4
Federal Nat'l. Mtg.	4.375-96	8-78	92.00	4-79	81.88	8	−10
Host International	5.25 -94	8-78	76.25	9-78	79.00	1	+ 2
Chromalloy American	$ 5.00 pfd.	8-78	77.25	3-79	76.33	7	0
Holiday Inns	$ 1.70 pfd.	8-78	30.38	12-78	29.62	4	− 4
Woolworth	$ 2.20 pfd.	8-78	30.00	4-79	42.00	8	+41
Reserve Oil & Gas	$ 1.75 pfd.	8-78	23.88	3-79	24.88	7	+ 4
U.S. Gypsum	$ 1.80 pfd.	8-78	29.50	8-79	32.00	12	+10
Amfac	$ 1.00 pfd.	8-78	12.75	12-79	14.25	16	+16
Grace (W.R.)	6.50 -92	9-78	96.50	11-78	100.50	2	+ 3
Owens-Illinois	4.50 -92	9-78	84.62	12-78	69.50	3	−19
Bally Manufacturing	6.00 -98	9-78	100.00	12-78	83.25	3	−17
Amerada Hess	$ 3.50 pfd.	9-78	66.58	12-78	63.00	3	− 7
TRW Corp.	$ 4.50 pfd.	9-78	75.00	4-79	72.00	7	− 3
Brunswick	$ 2.40 pfd.	10-78	33.88	12-78	28.25	2	−18
Travelers	$ 2.00 pfd.	11-78	35.25	1-79	39.50	2	+ 9
I.U. International	$ 1.36 pfd.	11-78	14.00	4-79	14.88	5	+ 7

Company		Rate						
Carrier		5.125-89	12-78	91.50	7-79	97.73	7	+ 8
Textron	$	2.08 pfd.	1-79	28.50	1-80	31.62	12	+14
INA Corp.	$	1.90 pfd.	1-79	22.75	9-80	31.25	20	+48
Tandy		6.50 -03	2-79	104.00	4-79	98.00	2	− 7
Bally Manufacturing		6.00 -98	2-79	106.00	3-79	115.00	1	+ 7
Amerada Hess	$	3.500 pfd.	2-79	57.50	2-79	62.00	1	+ 5
Crocker National	$	3.00 pfd.	2-79	41.50	12-79	43.00	8	+ 6
Brunswick	$	2.40 pfd.	2-79	28.50	5-81	34.75	27	+36
Amax	$	3.00 pfd.	3-79	46.75	6-79	54.00	3	+14
Arvin Industries	$	2.00 pfd.	3-79	25.00	4-81	25.78	25	+15
International Tel. & Tel.	$	4.00 pfd.	4-79	46.00	8-80	48.97	16	+15
FMC Corp.		4.25 -92	5-79	73.50	9-79a	76.12	4	+ 3
Burlington Northern		5.25 -92	5-79	89.00	6-79	105.00	1	+16
Greyhound		6.50 -90	5-79	88.00	12-80	80.00	19	0
Washington National	$	2.50 pfd.	5-79	38.50	9-79a	39.38	4	+ 2
Armco Steel	$	2.10 pfd.	5-79	27.25	10-79	31.12	5	+13
Carter Hawley Hale	$	2.00 pfd.	5-79	27.25	10-79	31.00	5	+13
Pitney-Bowes	$	2.12 pfd.	5-79	29.00	6-80	38.00	13	+34
Woolworth	$	2.20 pfd.	6-79	37.00	9-79a	40.50	3	+ 7
Alum. Co. America		5.25 -91	7-79	95.25	2-80	112.00	7	+19
Dayco		6.00 -94	7-79	79.50	7-80	68.12	12	− 9
Insilco	$	1.25 pfd.	7-79	16.12	6-80b	17.00	11	+ 9
Phillips-Van Heusen		5.25 -94	8-79	64.00	9-79a	62.00	1	− 6
BanCal Tri-State		6.50 -96	9-79b	81.25	6-80	99.12	9	+25
Ford Motor		4.50 -96	9-79b	68.50	12-79	55.38	3	−20
Lone Star Industries		5.125-93	9-79b	95.00	12-79	96.00	3	0
North Amer. Philips		4.00 -92	9-79b	70.00	11-80	75.93	14	+12
McDonnell Douglas		4.75 -92	9-79b	91.00	11-79	95.00	2	+ 3
Riegel Textile		5.00 -93	9-79b	70.50	3-80	72.75	6	+ 4
Walter, Jim		5.75 -91	9-79b	87.50	1-80	81.75	4	− 7

Company	Convertible description	Purchase data		Sale data		Months held	Net total return
		Date	Price	Date	Price		
SCM Corp.	5.50 -88	9-79b	80.50	1-80	73.50	4	— 9
Amerace	$ 2.60 pfd.	9-79b	43.25	10-79	44.25	1	— 1
Arcata	$ 2.16 pfd.	9-79b	28.75	4-80	28.75	7	0
GK Technologies	$ 1.94 pfd.	9-79b	27.25	11-79	28.38	2	+ 1
RCA Corp.	$ 4.00 pfd.	9-79b	54.00	2-80	51.00	5	— 5
United Technologies	$ 7.32 pfd.	9-79b	111.00	12-79	114.00	3	+ 3
Western Union	$ 4.90 pfd.	9-79b	54.00	6-80b	59.00	9	+13
Ford Motor	4.875-98	12-79	58.88	5-80	53.25	5	— 9
Cooper Industries	$ 2.90 pfd.	12-79	37.25	6-80	41.25	6	+11
Reynolds Metals	4.50 -91	1-80	71.92	6-80	69.00	5	— 4
Georgia Pacific	$ 2.24 pfd.	1-80	31.75	open			
RCA Corp.	$ 2.125 pfd.	2-80	19.25	6-80	21.50	4	+13
Gulf & Western	5.50 -93	4-80	87.50	6-80b	100.00	2	+13
Federal Nat'l. Mtg.	4.375-96	4-80	73.50	5-80	86.00	1	+15
Foremost McKesson	6.00 -94	4-80	75.00	5-80	88.00	1	+15
McDonnell Douglas	4.75 -92	5-80	93.25	10-80	110.00	5	+18
Bally Manufacturing	6.00 -98	5-80	95.00	7-80	107.00	2	+12
Natomas	$ 4.00 pfd.	5-80	58.50	6-80	64.75	1	+ 8
United Technologies	$ 3.875 pfd.	5-80	51.00	8-80	63.25	3	+22
Crocker National	5.75 -96	6-80	70.00	12-80	85.00	6	+21
Owens-Illinois	4.50 -92	6-80	82.00	2-81	96.00	8	+18
FMC Corp.	4.24 -92	6-80c	66.50	12-80	75.25	6	+13
Tyco Laboratories	5.875-91	6-80c	89.25	9-80	113.77	3	+27
Walter, Jim	5.75 -91	6-80c	85.00	7-80	89.50	1	+ 4
Phillips-Van Heusen	5.25 -94	6-80c	55.75	8-80	64.00	2	+13

Company		Date	Price	Date	Price	No.	Change
RCA Corp.	$ 4.00 pfd.	6-80	50.00	8-80	57.25	2	+11
Washington	$ 2.50 pfd.	6-80c	37.00	8-80	42.97	2	+12
Bendix	$ 4.04 pfd.	6-80c	41.00	8-80	44.75	2	+7
Western Union	$ 4.60 pfd.	6-80c	51.75	9-80	59.88	3	+15
I.C. Industries	$ 3.50 pfd.	7-80	40.94	8-80	46.12	1	+9
Citicorp	5.75 -00	8-80	66.90	4-81	69.00	8	+6
Gulf United	9.25 -05	8-80	100.25	4-81	98.75	8	+3
RCA Corp.	$ 2.125 pfd.	9-80	22.88	10-80	24.00	1	+2
Reynolds Metals	4.50 -91	10-80	71.25	9-81	66.00	11	−4
Bally Manufacturing	6.00 -98	11-80	85.62	5-81	101.50	6	+19
Wang Labs	9.00 -05	12-80	121.50	5-81	133.00	5	+11
Household Finance	$ 2.50 pfd.	12-80	25.75	3-81	27.38	3	+5
Signal Companies	5.50 -94	12-80	84.50	open			
RCA Corp.	$ 2.125 pfd.	2-81	22.50	11-80	16.25	9	−24
Walter, Jim	5.75 -91	3-81	74.00	8-81	73.50	5	0
Edwards, A.G.	10.50 -06	3-81	103.42	open			
Moog	9.875-06	4-81	116.00	open			
Dean Witter Reynolds	10.00 -05	4-81	113.00	12-81	183.15	8	+66
Storage Technology	10.25 -00	4-81	119.00	10-81	149.50	6	+28
Trinity Industries	10.00 -06	5-81	100.50	open			
Hutton, E.F.	9.50 -05	6-81	109.00	open			
U.S. Air	8.25 -05	7-81	104.00	open			
Tiger International	8.625-05	8-81	78.00	open			
Hospital Corp. of Amer.	8.75 -06	9-81	102.00	open			
Nat'l. Medical Enterpr.	9.00 -06	9-81	74.00	10-81	86.20	1	+15
Holiday Inns	9.625-05	9-81	116.50	open			
Oak Industries	11.00 -00	9-81	110.00	10-81	135.00	1	+22
Ralston Purina	5.75 -00	10-81	74.00	open			

APPENDIX C *(concluded)*

Company	Convertible description	Purchase data		Sale data		Months held	Net total return
		Date	Price	Date	Price		
Merrill Lynch............	9.25 -00	11-81	103.60	open			
Allied Chemical	7.75 -00	11-81	84.00	open			
RCA Corp.	$ 4.00 pfd.	11-81	40.44	open			
Nat'l. Medical Enterpr.	9.00 -06	11-81	80.00	open			
Reading & Bates	$ 2.125 pfd.	11-81	33.00	open			
Ashland Oil	$ 3.96 pfd.	11-81	38.25	open			

Note: This table presents low-risk convertibles purchased for the author's largest managed accounts beginning late 1975. The term *low-risk* is defined as convertibles whose underlying common stocks were rated B+ or higher by Standard & Poor's or high quality financial stocks not rated by S&P. The net total return figures include income received, capital gain or loss, and roundtrip commissions. Where an account was replaced by a new larger account, end of the quarter prices were used to close out an older convertible not held by the new account or to establish starting prices for convertibles held by the new account not held by the former. These are shown by **a**, **b**, or **c** for the three clients involved in the study.

APPENDIX D

Quarterly returns for all undervalued convertibles evaluated during the six-year study, 1976 through 1981

The performance data presented in Table D-1 assumed equal dollar investments were made in each convertible, adjusted quarterly. Detailed calculations for the analysis of the All-convertibles group are presented in Tables D-2 through D-25.

TABLE D-1
Quarterly returns for convertibles purchased over the six-year period

Year and quarter	Low-risk convertibles		Aggressive convertibles		All-convertibles	
	Quarter	Annual	Quarter	Annual	Quarter	Annual
1976- 1	+18.0%		+ 9.7%		+15.2%	
2	+ 4.9		+ 9.0		+ 6.2	
3	+ 5.5		+ 6.1		+ 5.6	
4	+ 6.1	+ 38.6%	+ 4.9	+ 33.1%	+ 5.6	+ 36.4%
1977- 1	- 1.4		+ 1.5		- 0.8	
2	+ 6.2		+ 4.9		+ 6.0	
3	- 1.3		+ 0.5		- 0.8	
4	+ 1.4	+ 4.8	+ 1.9	+ 9.0	+ 1.6	+ 6.0
1978- 1	+ 2.4		+10.6		+ 5.3	
2	+11.1		+10.4		+10.9	
3	+ 8.1		+14.7		+10.0	
4	- 9.8	+ 10.9	- 6.9	+ 30.4	- 9.2	+ 16.7
1979- 1	+ 9.3		+13.9		+10.5	
2	+ 6.8		+ 8.4		+ 7.2	
3	+ 6.0		+ 8.5		+ 6.6	
4	- 3.1	+ 19.9	+ 2.1	+ 36.8	- 1.9	+ 23.9
1980- 1	- 6.5		- 4.2		- 5.8	
2	+20.7		+15.7		+19.0	
3	+14.2		+11.2		+13.3	
4	+ 0.2	+ 29.1	+ 7.2	+ 32.1	+ 3.7	+ 31.7
1981- 1	+ 7.6		+11.8		+ 9.9	
2	+ 4.8		+ 1.5		+ 2.7	
3	- 9.9		-12.1		-11.4	
4	+10.9	+ 12.7	+ 4.7	+ 4.4	+ 6.9	+ 6.9
Cumulative return (six years)		+181.0%		+256.9%		+194.1%

1976—First quarter ending March 31

Convertible	(1) Starting price	(2) Opening price	(3) Closing price	(4) Ending price	(5) Gain or loss
Chase Manhattan	61.00			68.00	+ 11.5%
Federal Nat'l. Mtg.	77.75		82.00		+ 5.5
Gulf & Western	82.00		95.50		+ 16.5
Internat'l. Tel. & Tel.	41.00		45.00		+ 9.8
Occidental Petroleum	46.88			49.75	+ 6.1
Pan American	78.00			90.00	+ 15.4
Tesoro Petroleum	82.75			94.12	+ 13.7
United Technologies	66.50			78.50	+ 18.0
El Paso		83.00		82.38	− 0.8
Greyhound		82.25		92.62	+ 12.6
Total					+108.3%
Average gain or loss = +108.3 ÷ 7.5*					+ 14.4%
Income received†					+ 1.8
Commissions paid = 1.5 × 5 ÷ 7.5‡					− 1.0
Net gain or loss					+ 15.2%

*Average gain or loss equals the total gain or loss (+108.3 percent from column 5) divided by the average of the starting number of positions (8 from column 1) and the ending number (7 from column 4) or 7.5.

†Income received for the quarter equals the average current yield for the portfolio (7.2 percent) divided by 4.

‡Commissions paid equal 1.5 percent per transaction times the number of trades (two new positions opened from Column 2 plus three positions closed out from column 3) divided by the average number of positions (7.5).

TABLE D-3
1976—Second quarter ending June 30

	(1) Starting price	(2) Opening price	(3) Closing price	(4) Ending price	(5) Gain or loss
Chase Manhattan	68.00		68.25		+ 0.4%
El Paso	82.38			81.50	− 1.1
Greyhound	92.62			92.00	− 0.7
Occidental Petroleum	49.75		57.25		+15.1
Pan American	90.00		92.75		+ 3.1
Tesoro Petroleum	94.12			90.12	− 4.2
United Technologies	78.50		88.25		+12.4
Federal Nat'l. Mtg.		72.75		74.50	+ 2.4
Grace		94.12		95.50	+ 1.5
Internat'l. Tel. & Tel.		31.25		34.62	+10.8
Total					+39.7%
Average gain or loss = +39.7 ÷ 6.5					+ 6.1%
Income received					+ 1.7
Commissions paid = 1.5 X 7 ÷ 6.5					− 1.6
Net gain or loss					+ 6.2%

TABLE D-4
1976—Third quarter ending September 30

	(1) Starting price	(2) Opening price	(3) Closing price	(4) Ending price	(5) Gain or loss
El Paso	81.50			85.00	+ 4.3%
Federal Nat'l. Mtg.	74.50			83.00	+11.4
Grace	95.50			99.50	+ 4.2
Greyhound	92.00		90.75		– 1.4
Internat'l. Tel. & Tel.	34.62		38.62		+11.6
Tesoro Petroleum	90.12			88.00	– 2.4
Ford Motor		82.50		87.00	+ 5.5
Woolworth		35.00		33.75	–3.6
Total					+29.6%
Average gain or loss = +29.6 ÷ 6					+ 4.9%
Income received					+ 1.7
Commissions paid = 1.5 X 4 ÷ 6					– 1.0
Net gain or loss					+ 5.6%

TABLE D-5

1976—Fourth quarter ending December 31

	(1) Starting price	(2) Opening price	(3) Closing price	(4) Ending price	(5) Gain or loss
El Paso	85.00			88.00	+ 3.5%
Federal Nat'l. Mtg.	83.00		80.75	89.00	− 2.7
Ford Motor	87.00			89.00	+ 2.3
Grace	99.50		99.50		0
Tesoro Petroleum	88.00			96.00	+ 9.1
Woolworth	33.75		37.50		+11.1
Avco		103.50	106.00		+ 2.4
Budd Company		91.88		95.50	+ 3.9
Gulf & Western		90.75		95.00	+ 4.7
Pan American		76.25		79.00	+ 3.6
Riegel Textile		77.50		80.00	+ 3.2
Wallace Murray		100.00		101.50	+ 1.5
Total					+42.6%
Average gain or loss = +42.6 ÷ 7					+ 6.1%
Income received					+ 1.6
Commissions paid = 1.5 × 10 ÷ 7					− 2.1
Net gain or loss					+ 5.6%

Note: Twelve convertibles purchased in December were excluded to avoid distortion of the quarterly results. These are identified with an * in the next table.

TABLE D-6
1977—First quarter

	(1) Starting price	(2) Opening price	(3) Closing price	(4) Ending price	(5) Gain or loss
Airco*	95.75			96.00	+ 0.3%
American Hoist*	91.88			109.50	+19.2
Beech Aircraft*	84.75			78.00	− 8.0
Budd Company	95.50			90.00	− 5.8
Continental Telephone*	84.12			83.25	− 1.0
El Paso	88.00		93.00		+ 5.7
Federal Nat'l. Mtg.*	85.62			79.50	− 7.2
Ford Motor	89.00			83.50	− 6.2
GAF Corp.*	19.38		18.69		− 3.6
Gulf & Western	95.00			82.00	−13.7
Hilton Hotels*	86.00			81.00	− 5.8
National Distillers*	99.62			98.00	− 1.6
North Amer. Philips*	78.00			76.00	− 2.6
Pan American	79.00		76.88		− 2.7
Parker Hannifan*	74.62			77.00	+ 3.2
Riegel Textile	80.00			74.00	− 7.5
Storer Broadcasting*	85.00			87.50	+ 2.9
Tesoro Petroleum	96.00		102.00		+ 6.2
U. V. Industries*	81.25			85.75	+ 5.5
Wallace Murray	101.50		118.00		+16.3
Citicorp		94.50		89.25	− 5.6
City Investing		99.50		98.00	− 1.5
E-Systems		86.25		89.00	+ 3.2
Grumman		61.50		60.75	− 1.2

TABLE D-6 *(continued)*

	(1) Starting price	(2) Opening price	(3) Closing price	(4) Ending price	(5) Gain or loss
Houston Industries		94.50		95.00	+ 0.5%
Melville		89.00		87.50	− 1.7
Ogden		71.00		71.50	+ 0.7
Sola Basic		90.12		90.00	− 0.1
Tesoro Petroleum		94.00		83.00	−11.7
White Consolidated		101.50		102.75	+ 1.2
Zapata		70.91		65.00	− 8.3
Total					−30.9%
Average gain or loss = −30.9 ÷ 23					− 1.3%
Income received					+ 1.5
Commissions paid = 1.5 × 16 ÷ 23					− 1.0
Net gain or loss					− 0.8%

TABLE D-7
1977—Second Quarter

	(1) Starting price	(2) Opening price	(3) Closing price	(4) Ending price	(5) Gain or loss
Airco	96.00		105.00		+ 9.4%
American Hoist	109.50		123.00		+ 12.3
Beech Aircraft	78.00			86.50	+ 10.9
Budd Company	90.00			92.25	+ 2.5
Citicorp	89.25			87.00	− 2.5
City Investing	98.00		104.75		+ 6.9
Continental Telephone	83.25			84.75	+ 1.8
E-Systems	89.00			96.00	+ 7.9
Federal Nat'l. Mtg.	79.50			84.12	+ 5.8
Ford Motor	83.50			84.50	+ 1.2
Grumman	60.75		69.75		+ 14.8
Gulf & Western	82.00		78.25		− 4.6
Hilton Hotels	81.00		87.00		+ 7.4
Houston Industries	95.00			98.00	+ 3.2
Melville	87.50			85.50	− 2.3
National Distillers	98.00			94.75	− 3.3
North Amer. Philips	76.00		77.39		+ 1.8
Ogden	71.50			73.00	+ 2.1
Parker Hannifan	77.00		87.00		+ 13.0
Riegel Textile	74.00			74.50	+ 0.7
Sola Basic	90.00		120.00		+ 33.3
Storer Broadcasting	87.50		86.12		− 1.6
Tesoro Petroleum	83.00			85.00	+ 2.4
U. V. Industries	85.75			90.75	+ 5.8
White Consolidated	102.75		106.50		+ 3.6

TABLE D-7 *(continued)*

	(1) Starting price	(2) Opening price	(3) Closing price	(4) Ending price	(5) Gain or loss
Zapata	65.00			67.50	+ 3.8%
Arvin Industries		28.00		28.88	+ 3.1
Avco		114.50		116.00	+ 1.3
Castle & Cooke		79.00		79.38	+ 0.5
Curtis Wright		27.25		27.25	0
Dayco		93.00		93.50	+ 0.5
Harrah's		111.50		112.00	+ 0.4
Lear Siegler		41.00		41.38	+ 0.9
Oak Industries		70.00	72.00		+ 2.9
Pan American		88.50		87.75	− 0.8
Woolworth		34.50		34.00	− 1.4
Total					+143.7%
Average gain or loss = +143.7 ÷ 25 ...					+ 5.7%
Income received					+ 1.6
Commissions paid = 1.5 X 22 ÷ 25 ...					− 1.3
Net gain or loss					+ 6.0%

TABLE D-8
1977—Third quarter

	(1) Starting price	(2) Opening price	(3) Closing price	(4) Ending price	(5) Gain or loss
Arvin Industries	28.88			30.50	+ 5.6%
Avco	116.00			109.50	− 5.6
Beech Aircraft	86.50			98.00	+13.3
Budd Company	92.25			96.50	+ 4.6
Castle & Cooke	79.38			80.00	+ 0.8
Citicorp	87.00			83.00	− 4.6
Continental Telephone	84.75		85.25	27.00	+ 0.6
Curtis Wright	27.25			90.00	− 0.9
Dayco	93.50			82.62	− 3.7
E-Systems	96.00			83.00	−13.9
Federal Nat'l. Mtg.	84.12			83.75	− 1.3
Ford Motor	84.50			106.50	− 0.9
Harrah's	112.00			93.00	− 4.9
Houston Industries	98.00			38.00	− 5.1
Lear Siegler	41.38			90.00	− 8.2
Melville	85.50			91.25	+ 5.3
National Distillers	94.75			68.62	− 3.7
Ogden	73.00			84.50	− 6.0
Pan American	87.75			73.12	− 3.7
Riegel Textile	74.50				− 1.8
Tesoro Petroleum	85.00		80.00		− 5.9
U. V. Industries	90.75			96.50	+ 6.3
Woolworth	34.00			28.88	−15.1
Zapata	67.50		70.94		+ 5.1
Grumman		111.00		105.00	− 5.4
Total					−49.1%

Average gain or loss = −49.1 ÷ 23 .... − 2.1%
Income received .... + 1.6
Commissions paid = 1.5 × 4 ÷ 23 .... − 0.3
Net gain or loss .... − 0.8%

TABLE D-9
1977—Fourth quarter

	(1) Starting price	(2) Opening price	(3) Closing price	(4) Ending price	(5) Gain or loss
Arvin Industries	30.50			29.88	− 2.0%
Avco	109.50			115.75	+ 5.7
Beech Aircraft	98.00		96.00		− 2.0
Budd Company	96.50			108.50	+12.4
Castle & Cooke	80.00			90.88	+13.6
Citicorp	83.00			78.00	− 6.0
Curtis Wright	27.00		26.00		− 3.7
Dayco	90.00			86.25	− 4.2
E-Systems	82.62		84.00		+ 1.7
Federal Nat'l. Mtg.	83.00			76.50	− 7.8
Ford Motor	83.75			82.25	− 1.8
Grumman	105.00			103.50	− 1.4
Harrah's	106.50			108.25	+ 1.6
Houston Industries	93.00			90.50	− 2.7
Lear Siegler	38.00			41.12	+ 8.2
Melville	90.00			94.50	+ 5.0
National Distillers	91.25		87.25		− 4.4
Ogden	68.62			70.12	+ 2.2
Pan American	84.50			83.50	− 1.2
Riegel Textile	73.12			74.50	+ 1.9
U. V. Industries	96.50			92.00	− 4.7
Woolworth	28.88		30.00		+ 3.9
Amerada Hess		62.88		62.75	− 0.2
Cooper Laboratories		66.50		66.00	− 0.8

Foremost McKesson	28.83	29.25	+ 1.5
Gulf & Western	30.25	30.25	0
Hilton Hotels	86.75	91.00	+ 4.9
National City Lines	70.00	65.25	− 6.8
Pennwalt	23.50	24.25	+ 3.2
Republic N.Y.	74.50	77.00	+ 3.4
Texasgulf	39.50	39.25	− 0.6
Total			+18.9%

Average gain or loss = +18.9 ÷ 24 .... + 0.8%

Income received .... + 1.7

Commissions paid = 1.5 × 14 ÷ 24 .... − 0.9

Net gain or loss .... + 1.6%

TABLE D-10
1978—First quarter

	(1) Starting price	(2) Opening price	(3) Closing price	(4) Ending price	(5) Gain or loss
Amerada Hess ················	62.75			57.50	− 8.4%
Arvin Industries ·············	29.88			29.00	− 2.9
Avco ·····················	115.75			132.75	+ 14.7
Budd Company ··············	108.50		142.00		+ 30.9
Castle & Cooke ·············	90.88			87.75	− 3.4
Citicorp ··················	78.00		75.12		− 3.7
Cooper Laboratories ·········	66.00			71.25	+ 8.0
Dayco ····················	86.25			89.00	+ 3.2
Federal Nat'l. Mtg. ··········	76.50			72.25	− 5.6
Ford Motor ················	82.25			82.75	+ 0.6
Foremost McKesson ··········	29.25			28.25	− 3.4
Grumman ·················	103.50			99.50	− 3.9
Gulf & Western ·············	30.25			32.25	+ 6.6
Harrah's ··················	108.25			119.00	+ 9.9
Hilton Hotels ··············	91.00			102.38	+ 12.5
Houston Industries ··········	90.50			87.62	− 3.2
Lear Siegler ···············	41.12		37.75		− 8.2
Melville ··················	94.50			91.00	− 3.7
National City Lines ··········	65.25			70.25	+ 7.7
Ogden ···················	70.12		69.00		− 1.6
Pan American ··············	83.50			89.25	+ 6.9
Pennwalt ··················	24.25			23.38	− 3.6
Republic N.Y. ··············	77.00			79.50	+ 3.2
Riegel Textile ··············	74.50			78.75	+ 5.7
Texasgulf Inc. ·············	39.25			38.25	− 2.5

U.V. Industries	92.00			91.00	− 1.1
Beech Aircraft		91.00	102.00		+ 12.1
Carrier		27.75		31.25	+ 12.6
Chromalloy American		63.00		69.88	+ 10.9
Holiday Inns		24.50		26.00	+ 6.1
Kaiser Cement		34.62		38.62	+ 11.6
Total					+108.0%
Average gain or loss = +108.0 ÷ 26					+ 4.2%
Income received					+ 1.7
Commissions paid = 1.5 X 10 ÷ 26					− 0.6
Net gain or loss					+ 5.3%

TABLE D-11
1978—Second quarter

	(1) Starting price	(2) Opening price	(3) Closing price	(4) Ending price	(5) Gain or loss
Amerada Hess	57.50		64.00		+ 11.3%
Arvin Industries	29.00		33.40		+ 15.2
Avco	132.75			142.50	+ 7.3
Carrier	31.25		34.50		+ 10.4
Castle & Cooke	87.75			94.75	+ 8.0
Chromalloy American	69.88		92.79		+ 32.8
Cooper Laboratories	71.25			62.75	− 11.9
Dayco	89.00			92.50	+ 3.9
Federal Nat'l. Mtg.	72.25			89.00	+ 23.2
Ford Motor	82.75			84.25	+ 1.8
Foremost McKesson	28.25		34.25		+ 21.2
Grumman	99.50		109.25		+ 9.8
Gulf & Western	32.25		34.00		+ 5.4
Harrah's	119.00		147.00		+ 23.5
Hilton Hotels	102.38		115.00		+ 12.3
Holiday Inns	26.00		26.22		+ 0.8
Houston Industries	87.62			86.75	− 1.0
Kaiser Cement	38.62			39.50	+ 2.3
Melville.................	91.00		94.00		+ 3.3
National City Lines	70.25			61.00	− 13.2
Pan American	89.25			98.50	+ 10.4
Pennwalt	23.38			24.25	+ 3.7
Republic N.Y.	79.50		80.00		+ 14.5
Riegel Textile	78.75			91.00	+ 1.6
Texasgulf Inc.	38.25		38.50		+ 0.7

U. V. Industries	91.00		92.00	+ 1.1
Allegheny Airlines	131.00	182.00		+ 38.9
City Investing	101.25		100.75	− 0.5
Eastern Airlines	123.50		128.00	+ 3.6
GAF Corp.	16.42		18.38	+ 11.9
General Instrument	124.50		123.00	− 1.2
Gulf & Western	84.50		80.00	− 5.3
Household Finance	32.50		30.62	− 5.8
Humana	100.00		112.00	+ 12.0
McDermott	31.88		31.00	− 2.8
Phoenix Steel	84.00		80.50	− 4.2
Textron	23.50	26.66		+ 13.4
TRE Corp.	124.88		118.00	− 5.5
Western Airlines	80.00	104.00		+ 30.0
White Consolidated	90.50	91.00		+ 0.6
Wometco Enterprises	96.00		96.00	0
Zale	13.38		13.38	0
Total				+283.5%

Average gain or loss = +283.5 ÷ 25.5 ... + 11.1%
Income received ... + 1.7
Commissions paid = 1.5 X 33 ÷ 25.5 ... − 1.9
Net gain or loss ... + 10.9%

TABLE D-12
1978—Third quarter

	(1) Starting price	(2) Opening price	(3) Closing price	(4) Ending price	(5) Gain or loss
Avco	142.50		160.50		+ 12.6%
Castle & Cooke	94.75		110.50		+ 16.6
City Investing	100.75			102.00	+ 1.2
Cooper Laboratories	62.75			66.50	+ 6.0
Dayco	92.50			93.00	+ 0.5
Eastern Airlines	128.00		137.00		+ 7.0
Federal Nat'l. Mtg.	89.00		99.00		+ 11.2
Ford Motor	84.25		85.38		+ 1.3
GAF Corp.	18.38			18.38	0
General Instrument	123.00		132.75		+ 7.9
Gulf & Western	80.00			84.50	+ 5.6
Household Finance	30.62			33.62	+ 9.8
Houston Industries	86.75			90.00	+ 3.7
Humana	112.00		122.72		+ 9.6
Kaiser Cement	39.50		50.00		+ 26.6
National City Lines	61.00		60.00		— 1.6
McDermott	31.00		33.00		+ 6.5
Pan American	98.50		120.00		+ 21.8
Pennwalt	24.25		24.38		+ 0.5
Phoenix Steel	80.50			80.50	0
Republic N.Y.	91.00		91.00		0
TRE Corp.	118.00		126.00		+ 6.8
U.V. Industries	92.00		94.71		+ 2.9
Wometco Enterprises	96.00		111.00		+ 15.6
Zale	13.38		14.38		+ 7.5

Amerada Hess	66.58		72.25	+	8.5
Amfac	12.75		12.75		0
Bally Manufacturing	100.00		99.50	–	0.5
Carrier	33.75		49.00	+	45.2
Chromalloy American	77.25		85.00	+	10.0
Federal Nat'l. Mtg.	92.00		90.50	–	1.6
Fruefauf	76.50		79.25	+	3.6
Grace (W.R.)	96.50		99.50	+	3.1
Holiday Inns	30.38		28.25	–	7.0
Host International	76.25	79.00		+	3.6
Kaiser Cement	19.50		21.50	+	10.3
Litton Industries	70.00		75.00	+	7.1
Lone Star Industries	85.00		96.00	+	12.9
McDonnell Douglas	118.00		106.50	–	9.7
Mohawk Data Sciences	126.00	124.00		–	1.6
Owens-Illinois	84.62		81.00	–	4.3
Ramada Inns	126.00	159.00		+	26.2
Reserve Oil & Gas	23.88		23.88		0
Rockwell International	78.48		82.00	+	4.5
Storer Broadcasting	90.55		90.00	–	0.6
TRW Corp.	75.00		73.75	–	1.7
U.S. Gypsum	29.50		27.50	–	6.8
Woolworth	30.00		31.00	+	3.3
Total				+284.1%

Average gain or loss = +284.1 ÷ 26.5 .... + 10.7%

Income received .... + 1.7

Commissions paid = 1.5 × 43 ÷ 26.5 .... – 2.4

Net gain or loss .... + 10.0%

TABLE D-13
1978—Fourth quarter

	(1) Starting price	(2) Opening price	(3) Closing price	(4) Ending price	(5) Gain or loss
Amerada Hess	72.25		63.00		− 12.8%
Amfac	12.75			11.12	− 12.7
Bally Manufacturing	99.50		83.25		− 16.3
Carrier	49.00		50.21		+ 2.5
Chromalloy American	85.00			64.75	− 23.8
City Investing	102.00			87.50	− 14.2
Cooper Laboratories	66.50			58.00	− 12.8
Dayco	93.00			82.00	− 11.8
Federal Nat'l. Mtg. . . .	90.50			81.50	− 9.9
Fruehauf	79.25			66.50	− 16.1
GAF Corp.	18.38			15.50	− 15.6
Grace (W.R.)	99.50		100.50		+ 1.0
Gulf & Western	84.50			77.75	− 8.0
Holiday Inns	28.25		29.62		+ 4.9
Household Finance	33.62			29.75	− 11.5
Houston Industries	90.00			83.50	− 7.2
Kaiser Cement	21.50			19.38	− 9.9
Litton Industries	75.00			67.00	− 10.7
Lone Star Industries	96.00			85.00	− 11.5
McDonnell Douglas	106.50			110.50	+ 3.8
Owens-Illinois	81.00		69.50		− 14.2
Phoenix Steel	80.50			64.00	− 20.5
Reserve Oil & Gas	23.88			19.88	− 16.8
Rockwell International	82.00			76.62	− 6.6
Storer Broadcasting	90.00			94.62	+ 5.1

					Gain or Loss %
TRW Corp.	73.75			69.50	— 5.8
U.S. Gypsum	27.50			24.50	—10.9
Woolworth	31.00			27.50	—11.3
Brunswick		28.25	33.88		—16.6
Carrier			91.50	94.00	+ 2.7
Di Giorgio			74.50	76.25	+ 2.3
El Paso			90.25	90.00	— 0.3
I.U. International			14.00	13.88	— 0.9
Pan American		122.50	117.00		+ 4.7
Ramada Inns			117.00	113.75	— 2.8
Travelers			35.25	36.50	+ 3.5
Western Airlines			84.00	80.00	— 4.8
Total					—285.8%

Average gain or loss = −285.8 ÷ 28.5 .... — 10.0%

Income received .... + 1.7

Commissions paid = 1.5 × 17 ÷ 28.5 .... — 0.9

Net gain or loss .... — 9.2%

TABLE D-14
1979—First quarter

	(1) Starting price	(2) Opening price	(3) Closing price	(4) Ending price	(5) Gain or loss
Amfac	11.12			12.50	+ 12.4%
Carrier	94.00			93.00	− 1.1
Chromalloy American	64.75		76.33		+ 17.9
City Investing	87.50			99.75	+ 14.0
Cooper Laboratories	58.00			65.00	+ 12.1
Dayco	82.00			90.00	+ 9.8
Di Giorgio	76.25		82.00		+ 7.5
El Paso	90.00		102.00		+ 13.2
Federal Nat'l. Mtg.	81.50			81.00	− 0.6
Fruehauf	66.50			75.00	+ 12.8
GAF Corp.	15.50			16.25	+ 4.8
Gulf & Western	77.75			80.75	+ 3.9
Household Finance	29.75			29.88	+ 0.4
Houston Industries	83.50			85.50	+ 2.4
I.U. International	13.88			14.00	+ 0.9
Kaiser Cement	19.38			19.38	0
Litton Industries	67.00			72.00	+ 7.5
Lone Star Industries	85.00			89.38	+ 5.1
McDonnell Douglas	110.50		114.00		+ 3.2
Phoenix Steel	64.00		70.00		+ 9.4
Ramada Inns	113.75			149.00	+ 31.0
Reserve Oil & Gas	19.88		24.88		+ 25.2
Rockwell International	76.62		80.75		+ 5.4
Storer Broadcasting	94.62			96.00	+ 1.5
Travelers	36.50		39.50		+ 8.2

Stock					
TRW Corp.	69.50			67.25	− 3.2
U.S. Gypsum	24.50			26.00	+ 6.1
Western Airlines	80.00			84.50	+ 5.6
Woolworth	27.50			32.50	+ 18.2
Amax		46.75		50.38	+ 7.8
Amerada Hess		57.50	62.00		+ 7.8
Arvin Industries		25.00		24.88	− 0.5
Bally Manufacturing		106.00	115.00		+ 8.5
Brunswick		28.50		29.12	+ 2.2
Crocker National		41.50		43.00	+ 3.6
INA Corp.		22.75		24.12	+ 6.0
LTV Corp.		24.38		26.25	+ 7.7
Tandy		104.00		102.00	− 1.9
Textron		28.50		30.00	+ 5.3
Total					+280.2%

Average gain or loss = +280.2 ÷ 29 .... + 9.7%

Income received .... + 1.8

Commissions paid = 1.5 X 20 ÷ 29 .... − 1.0

Net gain or loss .... + 10.5%

TABLE D-15
1979—Second quarter

	(1) Starting price	(2) Opening price	(3) Closing price	(4) Ending price	(5) Gain or loss
Amfac	12.50			12.50	0%
Amax	50.38		54.00		+ 7.2
Arvin Industries	24.88			24.38	− 2.0
Brunswick	29.12			28.25	− 3.0
Carrier	93.00			94.75	+ 1.9
City Investing	99.75			104.25	+ 4.5
Cooper Laboratories	65.00			69.00	+ 6.2
Crocker National	43.00			46.00	+ 7.0
Dayco	90.00			95.12	+ 5.7
Federal Nat'l. Mtg.	81.00		81.88		+ 1.1
Fruehauf	75.00		83.00		+ 10.7
GAF Corp.	16.25			15.88	− 2.3
Gulf & Western	80.75			78.75	− 2.5
Household Finance	29.88			32.50	+ 8.8
Houston Industries	85.50			87.00	+ 1.8
INA Corp.	24.12			25.50	+ 5.7
I.U. International	14.00		14.88		+ 6.2
Kaiser Cement	19.38			20.50	+ 5.8
Litton Industries	72.00			80.50	+ 11.8
Lone Star Industries	89.38		95.00		+ 6.3
LTV Corp.	26.25			28.75	+ 9.5
Ramada Inns	149.00		173.50		+ 16.4
Storer Broadcasting	96.00		111.50		+ 16.1
Tandy	102.00		98.00		− 3.9
Textron	30.00			29.50	− 1.7

TRW Corp.	67.25	72.00		+ 7.1
U.S. Gypsum	26.00		26.12	+ 0.5
Western Airlines	84.50		78.25	− 7.4
Woolworth	32.50	42.00		+ 29.2
Armco Steel	27.25		28.62	+ 5.0
Burlington Northern	89.00	105.00		+ 18.0
Carter Hawley Hale	27.25		28.69	+ 5.3
FMC Corp.	73.50		75.75	+ 3.1
Greyhound	88.00		90.00	+ 2.3
Internat'l. Tel. & Tel.	46.00		47.25	+ 2.7
Pitney-Bowes	29.00		30.25	+ 4.3
Punta Gorda Isles	11.75		12.12	+ 3.2
Texasgulf Inc.	41.50		43.25	+ 4.2
Washington National	38.50		37.50	− 2.6
Woolworth	37.00		37.25	+ 0.7
Total				+192.9%

Average gain or loss = +192.9 ÷ 29 .... + 6.7%
Income received .... + 1.6
Commissions paid = 1.5 X 22 ÷ 29 ...... − 1.1
Net gain or loss .... + 7.2%

TABLE D-16
1979—Third quarter

	(1) Starting price	(2) Opening price	(3) Closing price	(4) Ending price	(5) Gain or loss
Amfac	12.50			14.12	+ 13.0%
Armco Steel	28.62			32.50	+ 13.5
Arvin Industries	24.38			24.25	− 0.5
Brunswick	28.25			28.00	− 0.9
Carrier	94.75		97.73		+ 3.1
Carter Hawley Hale	28.69			32.00	+ 11.5
City Investing	104.25		111.50		+ 7.0
Cooper Laboratories	69.00			63.50	− 8.0
Crocker National	46.00			46.75	+ 1.6
Dayco	95.12		100.00		+ 5.1
FMC Corp.	75.75			76.12	+ 0.5
GAF Corp.	15.88			15.88	0
Greyhound	90.00			84.62	− 6.0
Gulf & Western	78.75			83.88	+ 6.5
Household Finance	32.50			33.00	+ 1.5
Houston Industries	87.00			86.00	− 1.1
INA Corp.	25.50			25.00	− 2.0
Internat'l. Tel. & Tel.	47.25			45.75	− 3.2
Kaiser Cement	20.50		22.50		+ 9.8
Litton Industries	80.50			87.00	+ 8.1
LTV Corp.	28.75			27.38	− 4.8
Pitney-Bowes	30.25			32.00	+ 5.8
Punta Gorda Isles	12.12			12.88	+ 6.2
Texasgulf Inc.	43.25			50.75	+ 17.3
Textron	29.50			29.12	− 1.3

U.S. Gypsum	26.12	32.00		+ 22.5
Washington National	37.50	39.38		+ 5.0
Western Airlines	78.25	95.00		+ 21.4
Woolworth	37.25	40.50		+ 8.7
Alum. Co. America	95.25		105.50	+ 10.8
Conn. General Mtg.	81.00		78.50	− 3.1
Dayco	79.50		82.25	+ 3.5
Grumman	102.00		107.50	+ 5.4
Insilco	16.12		16.12	0
Phillips-Van Heusen	64.00		62.00	− 3.1
Total				+153.8%

Average gain or loss = +153.8 ÷ 29	+ 5.3%
Income received	+ 1.9
Commissions paid = 1.5 X 12 ÷ 29	− 0.6
Net gain or loss	+ 6.6%

TABLE D-17
1979—Fourth quarter

	(1) Starting price	(2) Opening price	(3) Closing price	(4) Ending price	(5) Gain or loss
Alum. Co. America	105.50			98.00	− 7.1%
Amfac	14.12		14.25		+ 0.9
Amerace	43.25		44.25		+ 2.3
Arcata	28.75			27.50	− 4.3
Armco Steel	32.50		31.12		− 4.2
Arvin Industries	24.25			20.38	− 16.0
BanCal Tri-State	81.25			96.00	+ 18.2
Brunswick	28.00			26.50	− 5.4
Carter Hawley Hale	32.00		31.00		− 3.1
Conn. General Mtg.	78.50			74.50	− 5.1
Crocker National	46.75		43.00		− 8.0
Dayco	82.25			70.50	− 14.3
Ford Motor	68.50		55.38		− 19.2
GAF Corp.	15.88			13.62	− 14.2
GK Technologies	27.25		28.38		+ 4.1
Greyhound	84.62			83.00	− 1.9
Grumman	107.50			123.00	+ 14.4
Gulf & Western	83.88			91.88	+ 9.5
Household Finance	33.00			27.88	− 15.5
Houston Industries	86.00			86.50	+ 0.6
INA Corp.	25.00			25.00	0
Insilco	16.12			15.62	− 3.1
Internat'l. Tel. & Tel.	45.75			42.00	− 8.2
Litton Industries	87.00			100.50	+ 15.5
Lone Star Industries	95.00		96.00		+ 1.1

LTV Corp.	27.38		25.88	— 5.5
McDonnell Douglas	91.00	95.00	88.00	+ 4.4
NFC Corp.	93.50		64.50	— 5.9
North Amer. Philips	70.00		32.50	— 7.9
Pitney-Bowes	32.00		49.38	+ 1.6
RCA Corp.	54.00		69.12	— 8.6
Riegel Textile	70.50		73.50	— 2.0
SCM Corp.	80.50		29.00	— 8.7
Texasgulf Inc.	50.75	50.25	45.75	— 1.0
Textron	29.12		80.00	— 0.4
Trans World	58.00		52.00	— 21.1
United Technologies	111.00	114.00		+ 2.7
Walter, Jim	87.50		36.25	— 8.6
Western Union	54.00		101.50	— 3.7
Cooper Industries	37.25		60.00	— 2.7
Fairmont Foods	94.62		71.00	+ 7.3
Ford Motor	58.88		48.12	+ 1.9
Sherwin Williams	71.00			0
UAL Corp.	55.00			— 12.5
Western Airlines	75.00	93.00		+ 24.0
Total				—109.7%

Average gain or loss = —109.7 ÷ 36 ..... — 3.0%

Income received .... + 1.9

Commissions paid = 1.5 X 18 ÷ 36 ..... — 0.8

Net gain or loss .... — 1.9%

TABLE D-18
1980—First quarter

	(1) Starting price	(2) Opening price	(3) Closing price	(4) Ending price	(5) Gain or loss
Alum. Co. America	98.00		112.00		+ 14.3%
Arcata	27.50			23.00	− 16.4
Arvin Industries	20.38			18.75	− 8.0
BanCal Tri-State	96.00			84.88	− 11.6
Brunswick	26.50			23.25	− 12.3
Conn. General Mtg.	74.50			61.00	− 18.1
Cooper Industries	36.25			34.88	− 3.8
Dayco	70.50			55.38	− 21.5
Fairmont Foods	101.50			87.00	− 14.3
Ford Motor	60.00			52.50	− 12.5
GAF Corp.	13.62			11.75	− 13.8
Greyhound	83.00			86.00	+ 3.6
Grumman	123.00		142.00		+ 15.4
Gulf & Western	91.88		105.00		+ 14.3
Household Finance	27.88			22.50	− 19.3
Houston Industries	86.50			78.88	− 8.8
INA Corp.	25.00			22.00	− 12.0
Insilco	15.62			14.88	− 4.8
Internat'l, Tel. & Tel.	42.00			38.12	− 9.2
Litton Industries	100.50			109.50	+ 9.0
LTV Corp.	25.88			27.75	+ 7.2
NFC Corp.	88.00			88.00	0
North Amer. Philips	64.50			55.62	− 13.8
Pitney-Bowes	32.50			29.88	− 8.1
RCA Corp.	49.38		51.00		+ 3.3

Stock	Cost	Sale	Cost	Sale	Gain/Loss
Riegel Textile	69.12	72.75			+ 5.2
SCM Corp.	73.50	73.50			0
Sherwin Williams	71.00			69.00	− 2.8
Textron	29.00	31.62			+ 9.1
Trans World	45.75			37.75	− 17.5
UAL Corp.	48.12			44.00	− 8.6
Walter, Jim	80.00	81.75			+ 2.2
Western Union	52.00			46.00	− 11.5
Georgia Pacific			31.75	27.50	− 13.4
Mattel			20.00	19.88	− 0.6
National Kinney			44.00	35.00	− 20.5
Phoenix Steel			65.00	60.00	− 7.7
RCA Corp.			19.25	18.38	− 4.5
Reynolds Metals			71.92	60.00	− 16.6
Sanders Associates			76.50	74.50	− 2.6
Total					−231.0%

Average gain or loss = −231.0 ÷ 32.5 . . . . . − 7.1%

Income received . . . . + 2.0

Commissions paid = 1.5 X 15 ÷ 32.5 . . . . − 0.7

Net gain or loss . . . . − 5.8%

TABLE D-19
1980—Second quarter

	(1) Starting price	(2) Opening price	(3) Closing price	(4) Ending price	(5) Gain or loss
Arcata	23.00		28.75		+ 25.0%
Arvin Industries	18.75			19.50	+ 4.0
BanCal Tri-State	84.88		99.12		+ 16.8
Brunswick	23.25			25.00	+ 7.5
Conn. General Mtg.	61.00			76.00	+ 24.6
Cooper Industries	34.88		41.25		+ 18.3
Dayco	55.38			60.50	+ 9.3
Fairmont Foods	87.00		106.00		+ 21.8
Ford Motor	52.50		53.25		+ 1.4
GAF Corp.	11.75			14.62	+ 24.5
Georgia Pacific	27.50			31.88	+ 15.9
Greyhound	86.00			88.00	+ 2.3
Household Finance	22.50			28.50	+ 26.7
Houston Industries	78.88			86.50	+ 9.7
INA Corp.	22.00			26.00	+ 18.2
Insilco	14.88			17.00	+ 14.3
Internat'l. Tel. & Tel.	38.12			44.50	+ 16.7
Litton Industries	109.50			115.00	+ 5.0
LTV Corp.	27.75		29.50		+ 6.3
Mattel	19.88		23.25		+ 17.0
National Kinney	35.00			38.50	+ 10.0
NFC Corp.	88.00			93.00	+ 5.7
North Amer. Philips	55.62			64.12	+ 15.3
Phoenix Steel	60.00		65.00		+ 8.3
Pitney-Bowes	29.88		38.00		+ 27.2

	Cost			% Gain/Loss
RCA Corp.	18.38	21.50		+ 17.0
Reynolds Metals	60.00	69.00		+ 15.0
Sanders Associates	74.50	82.50		+ 10.7
Sherwin Williams	69.00	73.00		+ 5.8
Trans World	37.75	44.00		+ 16.6
UAL Corp.	44.00		47.25	+ 7.4
Western Union	46.00		59.00	+ 28.3
Bally Manufacturing	95.00		103.00	+ 8.4
Crocker National	70.00		76.00	+ 8.6
Federal Nat'l. Mtg.	73.50	86.00		+ 17.0
Foremost McKesson	75.00	88.00		+ 17.3
Gulf & Western	87.50		100.00	+ 14.3
LTV Corp.	101.50		104.00	+ 2.5
McDonnell Douglas	93.25		100.75	+ 8.0
Natomas	58.50	64.75		+ 10.7
Owens-Illinois	82.00		81.38	− 0.8
Ozark Air Lines	64.75		68.00	+ 5.0
Ramada Inns	109.50		109.50	0
RCA Corp.	50.00		50.25	+ 0.5
United Technologies	51.00		53.88	+ 5.6
Total				+549.7%

Average gain or loss = +549.7 ÷ 30 .... + 18.3%

Income received .... + 2.2

Commissions paid = 1.5 X 30 ÷ 30 ...... − 1.5

Net gain or loss .... + 19.0%

TABLE D-20
1980—Third quarter

	(1) Starting price	(2) Opening price	(3) Closing price	(4) Ending price	(5) Gain or loss
Arvin Industries	19.50			24.00	+ 23.1%
Bally Manufacturing	103.00		107.00		+ 3.9
Bendix	41.00		44.75		+ 9.1
Brunswick	25.00			27.25	+ 9.0
Conn. General Mtg.	76.00			76.75	+ 1.0
Cooper Laboratories	64.75			75.00	+ 15.8
Crocker National	76.00			80.00	+ 5.3
Dayco	60.50		68.12		+ 12.6
FMC Corp.	66.50			71.00	+ 6.8
GAF Corp.	14.62		17.50		+ 19.7
Georgia Pacific	31.88			30.00	− 5.9
Greyhound	88.00			83.12	− 5.5
Houston Industries	86.50			80.00	− 7.5
INA Corp.	26.00		31.25		+ 20.2
Internat'l. Tel. & Tel.	44.50		48.97		+ 10.0
LTV Corp.	104.00			115.25	+ 10.8
McDonnell Douglas	100.75			120.00	+ 19.1
National Kinney	38.50		39.38		+ 2.3
NFC Corp.	93.00			117.50	+ 26.3
North Amer. Philips	64.12			72.00	+ 12.3
Owens-Illinois	81.38			80.00	− 1.7
Ozark Air Lines	68.00			87.00	+ 27.9
Phillips-Van Heusen	55.75		64.00		+ 14.8
Ramada Inns	109.50			120.75	+ 10.3

RCA Corp.	50.25	57.25		+ 13.9
Tyco Laboratories	89.25	113.77		+ 27.5
UAL Corp.	47.25		45.00	— 4.8
United Technologies	53.88	63.25		+ 17.4
Walter, Jim	85.00	89.50		+ 5.3
Warnaco	29.25		29.00	— 0.9
Washington National	37.00	42.97		+ 16.1
Western Union	51.75	59.88		+ 15.7
Allegheny Ludlum	95.80	100.00		+ 4.4
Citicorp	66.90		62.00	— 7.3
Grumman	117.00		113.62	— 2.9
Gulf United	100.25		102.00	+ 1.7
I.C. Industries	40.94	46.12		+ 12.7
RCA Corp.	22.88		23.00	+ 0.5
Total				+339.0%

Average gain or loss = +339.0 ÷ 27 .... + 12.6%

Income received .... + 1.9

Commissions paid = 1.5 X 22 ÷ 27 .... — 1.2

Net gain or loss .... + 13.3%

TABLE D-21
1980—Fourth quarter

	(1) Starting price	(2) Opening price	(3) Closing price	(4) Ending price	(5) Gain or loss
Arvin Industries	24.00			21.12	− 12.0%
Brunswick	27.25			27.62	+ 1.4
Citicorp	62.00			64.25	+ 3.6
Conn. General Mtg.	76.75		93.00		+ 21.2
Cooper Laboratories	75.00		84.60		+ 12.8
Crocker National	80.00		85.00		+ 6.2
FMC Corp.	71.00		75.25		+ 6.0
Georgia Pacific	30.00			30.00	0
Greyhound	83.12		80.00		− 3.8
Grumman	113.62			121.00	+ 6.5
Gulf United	102.00			92.50	− 9.3
Houston Industries	80.00		80.50		+ 0.6
LTV Corp.	115.25			167.00	+ 44.9
McDonnell Douglas	120.00		110.00		− 8.3
NFC Corp.	117.50		122.75		+ 4.5
North Amer. Philips	72.00		75.93		+ 5.5
Owens-Illinois	80.00			84.50	+ 5.6
Ozark Air Lines	87.00			78.00	− 10.3
Ramada Inns	120.75			105.00	− 13.0
RCA Corp.	23.00		24.00		+ 4.3
UAL Corp.	45.00			43.00	− 4.4
Warnaco	29.00			28.62	− 1.3
American Airlines		48.94		46.00	− 6.0
Ampex		77.50		84.50	+ 9.0

Bally Manufacturing	85.62	89.25	+ 4.2
Energy Resources	103.80	120.00	+ 15.6
Household Finance	25.75	24.00	− 6.8
Inexco Oil	119.50	121.00	+ 1.3
Reynolds Metals	71.25	65.75	− 7.7
U.S. Realty Investment	75.82	75.00	− 1.1
Wang Labs	121.50	130.25	+ 7.2
Western Union	56.25	51.38	− 8.7
Zenith Radio	102.00	104.00	+ 2.0
Total			+ 69.7%

Average gain or loss = +69.7 ÷ 22.5 . . . . + 3.1%

Income received . . . . + 2.0

Commissions paid = 1.5 X 21 ÷ 22.5 . . . . . − 1.4

Net gain or loss . . . . + 3.7%

TABLE D-22
1981—First quarter

	(1) Starting price	(2) Opening price	(3) Closing price	(4) Ending price	(5) Gain or loss
American Airlines	46.00		55.50		+ 20.7%
Arvin Industries	21.12			25.40	+ 20.2
Bally Manufacturing	89.25			83.00	— 7.0
Brunswick	27.62			29.88	+ 8.1
Citicorp	64.25			65.50	+ 1.9
Energy Resources	120.00			115.00	— 4.2
Georgia Pacific	30.00			34.25	+ 14.2
Grumman	121.00			117.00	— 3.3
Gulf United	92.50			99.00	+ 7.0
Household Finance	24.00		27.38		+ 14.1
Inexco Oil	121.00			116.88	— 3.4
LTV Corp.	167.00		198.35		+ 18.8
Owens-Illinois	84.50		96.00		+ 13.6
Ozark Air Lines	78.00			102.00	+ 30.8
Ramada Inns	105.00			120.00	+ 14.3
Reynolds Metals	65.75			70.00	+ 6.5
Signal Companies (Ampex)	84.50			85.50	+ 1.2
UAL Corp.	43.00			48.00	+ 11.6
U.S. Realty Investment	75.00			83.00	+ 10.7
Wang Labs	130.25			125.00	— 4.0
Warnaco	28.62		36.55		+ 27.7
Western Union	51.38			50.50	— 1.7
Zenith Radio	104.00			103.00	— 1.0
Columbia Pictures	104.00	104.00		111.00	+ 6.7

					Gain/Loss
Computer Sciences		83.00		80.50	− 3.0
Crystal Oil		112.58	150.00		+ 33.2
Edwards, A.G.		103.42		103.00	− 0.4
Instrument Systems		94.25		92.00	− 2.4
Macrodyne		108.00		111.50	+ 4.5
Newberry Energy		87.00		87.00	0
Prime Computer		130.00	112.50		− 13.5
RCA Corp.	22.50			21.75	− 3.3
Vishay Intertechnology		88.00		88.50	+ 0.6
Walter, Jim		74.00		75.00	+ 1.4
Total					+220.6%

Average gain or loss = +220.6 ÷ 25 . . . + 8.8%

Income received . . . . . + 2.2

Commissions paid = 1.5 X 18 ÷ 25 . . . − 1.1

Net gain or loss . . . . . + 9.9%

TABLE D-23
1981—Second quarter

	(1) Starting price	(2) Opening price	(3) Closing price	(4) Ending price	(5) Gain or loss
Arvin Industries	25.40		25.78		+ 1.5%
Bally Manufacturing	83.00		101.50		+22.3
Brunswick	29.88		34.75		+16.3
Citicorp	65.50		69.00		+ 5.3
Columbia Pictures	111.00			104.50	− 5.9
Computer Sciences	80.50			89.00	+10.6
Edwards, A. G.	103.00			112.00	+ 8.7
Energy Resources	115.00			102.50	−10.9
Georgia Pacific	34.25			32.50	− 5.1
Grumman	117.00			119.00	+ 1.7
Gulf United	99.00		98.75		− 0.3
Inexco Oil	116.88			106.00	− 9.3
Instrument Systems	92.00			79.00	−14.1
Macrodyne	111.50			111.50	0
Newberry Energy	87.00			84.00	− 3.4
Ozark Air Lines	102.00		130.64		+28.1
Ramada Inns	120.00		141.90		+18.2
RCA Corp.	21.75			20.00	− 8.0
Reynolds Metals	70.00			66.00	− 5.7
Signal Companies (Ampex) . . .	85.50			84.50	− 1.2
UAL Corp.	48.00			47.00	− 2.1
U.S. Realty Investment	83.00		88.48		+ 6.6
Vishay Intertechnology	88.50			82.00	− 7.3
Walter, Jim	75.00			75.12	+ 0.2
Wang Labs	125.00		133.00		+ 6.4

Western Union	50.50		50.50	0
Zenith Radio	103.00		104.00	+ 1.0
Dean Witter Reynolds	113.00		118.00	+ 4.4
Eastern Airlines	96.62		95.00	− 1.7
Energy Management	104.00		100.50	− 3.4
Fuqua Industries	75.00		75.00	0
GAF Corp.	15.75	18.94		+20.3
Health Chem	102.75		97.00	− 5.6
Hutton, E.F.	109.00		107.00	− 1.8
MGM Grand Hotels	79.23		84.75	+ 7.0
Moog	116.00		113.00	− 2.6
Prime Computer	124.00		124.50	+ 0.4
Punta Gorda Isles	73.50		74.00	+ 0.7
Recognition Equipment	115.00		102.00	−11.3
Sanders Associates	107.00		91.00	−15.0
Storage Technology	119.00		125.00	+ 5.0
TIE Communications	114.00		115.00	+ 0.9
Transtechnology	98.00		115.00	+ 1.5
Trans World	113.00		99.50	0
Trinity Industries	100.50		113.00	+ 1.0
Total			101.50	+53.4%

Average gain or loss = +53.4 ÷ 30.5 . . . . + 1.8%
Income received . . . . + 2.3
Commissions paid = 1.5 X 28 ÷ 30.5 . . . . . . − 1.4
Net gain or loss . . . . + 2.7%

TABLE D-24
1981—Third quarter

	(1) Starting price	(2) Opening price	(3) Closing price	(4) Ending price	(5) Gain or loss
Columbia Pictures	104.50			90.00	− 13.9%
Computer Sciences	89.00			69.50	− 21.9
Dean Witter Reynolds	118.00			97.00	− 17.8
Eastern Airlines	95.00			81.00	− 14.7
Edwards, A.G.	112.00			100.00	− 10.7
Energy Management	100.50			88.00	− 12.4
Energy Resources	102.50			88.00	− 14.1
Fuqua Industries	75.00			75.00	0
Georgia Pacific	32.50			26.25	− 19.2
Grumman	119.00			138.41	+ 16.3
Health Chem	97.00			72.00	− 25.8
Hutton, E.F.	107.00			105.25	− 1.6
Inexco Oil	106.00			102.50	− 3.3
Instrument Systems	79.00		79.50		+ 0.6
Macrodyne	111.50			83.00	− 25.6
MGM Grand Hotels	84.75			69.00	− 18.6
Moog	113.00			89.75	− 20.6
Newbery Energy	84.00			79.00	− 6.0
Prime Computer	124.50			88.75	− 28.7
Punta Gorda Isles	74.00			58.25	− 21.3
RCA Corp.	20.00			17.00	− 15.0
Recognition Equipment	102.00			80.00	− 21.6
Reynolds Metals	66.00		66.00		0
Sanders Associates	91.00			80.00	− 12.1
Signal Companies (Ampex)	84.50			75.00	− 11.2

Company	Buy	Sell	Gain/Loss %
Storage Technology	125.00	130.50	+ 4.4
TIE Communications	115.00	98.50	− 14.3
Transtechnology	99.50	79.00	− 20.6
Trans World	113.00	93.00	− 17.7
Trinity Industries	101.50	83.00	− 18.2
UAL Corp.	47.00	40.00	− 14.9
Vishay Intertechnology	82.00	71.00	− 13.4
Walter, Jim	75.12	73.50	− 2.2
Western Union	50.50	59.10	+ 11.7
Zenith Radio	104.00	74.00	− 28.8
Crystal Oil	104.50	109.50	+ 4.8
Fairfield Communities	107.08	93.00	− 13.1
Holiday Inns	116.50	118.00	+ 1.3
Hospital Corp. of America	102.00	102.50	+ 0.5
National Education	103.62	91.00	− 12.2
Nat'l. Medical Enterprises	74.00	75.00	+ 1.4
PSA Inc.	108.50	88.00	− 18.9
Ramada Inns	108.50	87.00	− 19.8
Tacoma Boatbuilding	95.50	87.00	− 8.9
Tiger International	78.00	64.50	− 17.3
U.S. Air	104.00	88.00	− 15.4
Total			−518.8%

Average gain or loss = −518.8 ÷ 39 ... − 13.3%
Income received ... + 2.4
Commissions paid = 1.5 X 14 ÷ 39 ... − 0.5
Net gain or loss ... − 11.4%

TABLE D-25
1981—Fourth quarter

	(1) Starting price	(2) Opening price	(3) Closing price	(4) Ending price	(5) Gain or loss
Columbia Pictures	90.00			113.12	+ 25.7%
Computer Sciences	69.50			65.12	− 6.3
Crystal Oil	109.50			104.50	− 4.6
Dean Witter Reynolds	97.00		183.00		+ 88.7
Eastern Airlines	81.00			74.50	− 8.0
Edwards, A. G.	100.00			117.00	+ 17.0
Energy Management	88.00			93.00	+ 5.7
Energy Resources	88.00			85.00	− 3.4
Fairfield Communities	93.00			100.00	+ 7.5
Fuqua Industries	75.00			99.25	+ 32.3
Georgia Pacific	26.25			26.75	+ 1.9
Grumman	138.41			117.75	− 14.9
Health Chem.	72.00			72.50	+ 0.7
Holiday Inns	118.00			138.00	+ 16.9
Hospital Corp. of America	102.50			100.00	+ 2.4
Hutton, E. F.	105.25			120.00	+ 14.0
Inexco Oil	102.50			103.25	+ 0.7
Macrodyne	83.00			82.00	− 1.2
MGM Grand Hotels	69.00			66.00	− 5.8
Moog	89.75			86.12	− 4.0
National Education	91.00			99.00	+ 8.8
Nat'l. Medical Enterprises	75.00		86.20		+ 14.9
Newberry Energy	79.00			75.00	− 5.1
Prime Computer	88.75		103.00		+ 16.1
PSA Inc.	88.00			85.50	− 2.8
Punta Gorda Isles	58.25			54.50	− 6.4
RCA Corp.	17.00		16.62		− 2.2
Ramada Inns	87.00			94.88	+ 9.1

Company				
Recognition Equipment	80.00		67.00	− 16.2
Sanders Associates	80.00		87.00	+ 8.8
Signal Companies (Ampex)	75.00		74.50	− 0.7
Storage Technology	130.50	149.50		+ 14.6
Tacoma Boatbuilding	87.00		100.50	+ 15.5
TIE Communications	98.50		110.00	+ 11.7
Tiger International	64.50		58.88	− 8.7
Transtechnology	79.00		87.00	+ 10.1
Trans World	93.00	96.00		+ 3.2
Trinity Industries	83.00		80.25	− 3.3
UAL Corp.	40.00	40.00		0
U.S. Air	88.00		80.00	− 9.1
Vishay Intertechnology	71.00		76.00	+ 7.0
Western Union	59.10	58.04		− 1.8
Zenith Radio	74.00		70.50	− 4.7
Allied Corp.	84.00		82.50	− 1.8
Brunswick	99.00		99.00	0
Galaxy Oil	100.00		86.50	− 13.5
Merrill Lynch	103.60		98.00	− 5.4
Oak Industries	110.00	135.00		+ 22.7
Pogo Producing	82.00		85.00	+ 3.7
Ralston Purina	74.00		77.50	+ 4.7
RCA Corp.	40.44		41.00	+ 1.4
Nat'l. Medical Enterprises	80.00		76.00	− 5.0
Reading & Bates	33.00		34.00	+ 3.0
Ashland Oil	38.25		36.00	− 5.9
Four-Phase Systems	91.12		87.00	− 4.5
Total				+218.7%

Average gain or loss = +218.7 ÷ 44.5 .... + 4.9%

Income received .... + 2.7

Commissions paid = 1.5 × 21 ÷ 44.5 .... − 0.7

Net gain or loss .... + 6.9%

CHAPTER 4

Hedging convertible bonds with common stock

Convertible bond hedging is a strategy consisting of the purchase of a convertible debenture and the sale of the related common stock against it. The technical term for the tactic is *covered short sale*. The objective when employing this strategy is to establish a very low-risk investment posture while seeking long-term capital appreciation. Appendix E following this chapter provides detailed information for readers new to short selling.

By protecting the convertible in declining markets, via profits earned from the short sale, hedging allows one to make good use of more volatile convertibles: convertibles associated with high-risk companies whose debt instruments may be of doubtful investment quality. Avoided by most investors, this group tends to be the most undervalued and thus offers the best opportunities.

Investors who would not usually consider owning aggressive convertibles can take advantage of their undervaluation through this low-risk hedging strategy. It is interesting to note that short selling, a highly speculative tactic when used alone, can be employed in combination with other tactics to produce the most conservative investment strategy.

Recognizing that hedging lowers profit potential in exchange for safety, the strategy can be employed as an alternative to money market instruments by long-term-oriented pension funds and other conservative investors. Experienced hedgers use the money market only when attractive hedging opportunities are temporarily unavailable.

The following guidelines should be carefully applied when selecting convertible bond hedge candidates.

1. The bond should be trading close to conversion value, thus offering most of the profit potential of its underlying stock.
2. The bond should be trading no more than about 50 percent over its investment value. This will limit its decline on a price drop by the common.
3. The common stock should pay little or no dividends since short sellers are obligated to pay any dividends declared. Bear in mind, a substantial yield advantage can provide good cash

flow while waiting for the hedge position to work out.

4. The stock should have a history of high volatility, indicating high probability for a major price move.

5. Both the bond and its common stock should be listed on the New York or American Stock Exchanges. I have used over-the-counter bonds in the past, and won't exclude them in the future; however, they usually have poor liquidity and are therefore difficult to buy or sell at favorable prices. *New convertibles* are the exception: when first issued, they trade over-the-counter for up to 30 days or longer. They should always be analyzed even though published data may not be readily available. Once the offering is complete, quick changes in the price relationship between the stock and the new issue frequently mean the convertible bonds become undervalued before being listed. At this time they usually attract broader interest by the investment public. This tends to price them more efficiently.

Convertible preferreds may also be considered for hedging, but when working in the secondary, lower-quality sector of the market, debt instruments assure the extra safety.

A hedge opportunity using a convertible bond of Energy Resources Corporation illustrates application of these guidelines. The following discourse demonstrates how the guidelines were employed in evaluating the bond's attractiveness as a hedging candidate. It also discusses how hedges can be adjusted to meet different investment objectives.

The Energy Resources 9s of 1995
convertible bond

Energy Resources is a small Dallas-based company having five principal lines of business: oil and gas exploration and development, heat treating, steel fabrication, air cleaning equipment, and uranium exploration. Revenues have grown from under $7 million in 1974 to about $18 million in 1980. The company is capitalized with 2.2 million common shares outstanding (about $33 million).

In January 1980, Energy Resources brought an \$8 million convertible debenture issue to the market for the purpose of reducing its bank indebtedness. Both the common stock and the bond are listed on the American Stock Exchange and are relatively active traders. The bond is convertible into 61.5 shares of stock (\$1,000 ÷ \$16.25 conversion price = 61.5 shares).

Trading at 100 with the common stock at \$15 (August 1980) the bond was a good candidate for hedging. Using the convertible price curve of Exhibit 4-1, a step-by-step evaluation along the previously established guidelines proceeded as follows:

1. *Upside potential.* Trading at a modest 9 percent premium over its conversion value of 92 (61.5 shares X \$15 per share = \$920), the bond offered most of the profit potential of the stock. As shown by Exhibit 4-1, if the common were to advance 50 percent from \$15.00 to \$22.50, the convertible bond should advance 40 percent from 100 to 140.
2. *Downside risk.* At 100, the bond was only 43 percent above its estimated investment value of 70. If the common stock were to decline 50 percent from \$15.00 to \$7.50, Exhibit 4-1 indicates that the bond would drop only about 22 percent (from 100 to 78).
3. *Yield advantage.* The bond's current yield of 9.0 percent, compared to 1.6 percent for the common, provided a generous yield advantage of 7.4 percent.
4. *Price volatility.* Although neither the *Value Line* nor the Merrill Lynch service provided a beta figure for Energy Resources, yearly lows and highs indicated it was a volatile stock.

	Low	High
1980	9⅞	23⅝
1979	6	14⅞
1978	5⅝	10½
1977	4⅞	8¾
1976	3⅝	7⅝

EXHIBIT 4-1
The convertible price curve for Energy Resources 9s of 1995
convertible bond, August 1980 (conversion ratio = 61.5 shares)

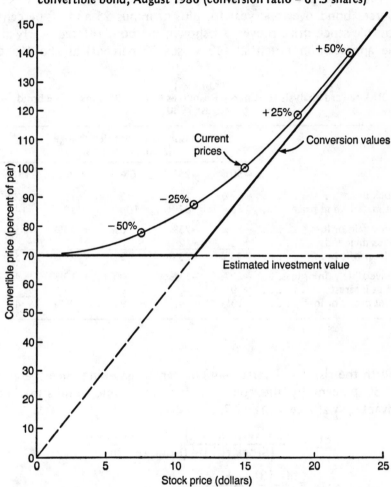

Risk-reward analysis

Table 4-1 presents a risk-reward analysis for the Energy Resources bond over one year for plus or minus 25 and 50 percent possible stock price moves. As shown, the bond offered nearly all the appreciation potential (49 versus 52 percent) at about one

TABLE 4-1
Risk-reward analysis for Energy Resources 9s of 1995 convertible bond,
August 1980

	Assumed stock price change (next 12 months)				
	−50%	−25%	0%	+25%	+50%
Stock price	7½	11¼	15	18¾	22½
Estimated bond price ...	78	87	100	119	140
Stock gain or loss	−50%	−25%	0%	+ 25%	+ 50
Plus dividends	+ 2	+ 2	+ 2	+ 2	+ 2
Net profit or loss	−48%	−23%	+ 2%	+ 27%	+ 52%
Convertible gain or loss. ...	−22%	−13%	0%	+ 19%	+ 40%
Plus interest	+ 9	+ 9	+ 9	+ 9	+ 9
Net profit or loss	−13%	− 4%	+ 9%	+ 28%	+ 49%

fourth the risk (−13 versus −48 percent). Assuming price changes of 50 percent by the common, the convertible bond's market advantage was a very high 1.7.

$$SE = \frac{(\text{Convertible risk}) - (\text{Bond return})}{(\text{Stock risk}) - (\text{Bond return})}$$

$$= \frac{(-13) - (+14)}{(-48) - (+14)}$$

$$= \frac{-27}{-62}$$

$$= .44$$

$$MA = \frac{(\text{Convertible return})}{.44(\text{Stock return}) + .56(\text{Bond return})}$$

$$= \frac{+52}{.44(+52) + .56(+14)}$$

$$MA = \frac{+52}{+22.9 + 7.0}$$

$$= \frac{+52}{+29.9}$$

$$= 1.74$$

In previous books I compared price moves of −50 percent and +100 percent since they more closely represent equal probabilities for future price action. (If a stock drops in half, it must later double in price to get back to the starting price; or if it first doubles, a 50 percent retracement would also bring it back to the starting price.) However, since I seldom hold a convertible at a price level much above 150, a 50 percent price advance is a more realistic target for most hedging situations.

Convertible hedge positions in
Energy Resources

By definition, the short sale of common stock against a convertible establishes a *convertible hedge position*. Since each Energy Resources 9s of 1995 was exchangeable into 61.5 shares of stock, the hedge could involve as little as one share or as many as 61.5 shares per bond. Throughout this entire range, (from 1 to 61.5) the stock sold short is considered a *covered* short sale. Unlike the high-risk market tactic of simply shorting stock and hoping for a price drop, covered short selling reduces risk. Up to the conversion ratio of 61.5 shares per bond, the higher the number of shares sold short, the lower the risk posture for the hedge position becomes.

Depending upon your personal investment goals, market outlook, and other securities in your portfolio, a convertible/stock hedge in Energy Resources could have been designed to meet a number of different objectives. By definition, the three basic convertible hedge strategies are:

1. *Partial hedge.* A bullish posture designed for upside profits at about break-even for a 50 percent stock price decline. About one third the number of shares into which the bond converts are sold short.

2. *Balanced hedge.* A **neutral** posture designed for modest profits regardless of which way the stock moves. Sell short about two thirds the number of shares into which the bond converts.
3. *Full hedge.* A bearish posture for downside profits at about upside break-even. Short nearly all the shares into which the bond converts.

Assuming the purchase of 10 Energy Resources bonds, representing 615 shares of common stock, hedge positions corresponding to the above alternatives are:

Partial hedge: 10 bonds versus 200 shares of stock sold short.
Balanced hedge: 10 bonds versus 400 shares of stock sold short.
Full hedge: 10 bonds versus 600 shares of stock sold short.

The profit and loss calculations for these three positions are presented in Table 4-2. Note that the cash investment of $10,000 is the same for each position since no additional cash (or collateral) is required for a covered short sale. Note also that the larger price moves of 50 percent are needed for meaningful profits, particularly after subtracting the cost of brokerage commissions, which are not included in these calculations. Exhibits 4-2 through 4-4 graphically illustrate the alternatives by plotting returns from Table 4-2 over a stock price range of $7.50 to $22.50 one year hence.

Managing a convertible bond hedge portfolio

As I illustrated with the Energy Resources example, hedge positions involving the short sale of common stock against significantly undervalued, aggressive convertible bonds is the safest form of investing known (excluding, of course, short-term money market instruments which are by definition risk-free). And yet hedging offers substantial opportunity for capital gain. It is a strategy that is ideally suited for conservative investors having long-range investment outlooks. However, it requires above-average expertise to identify acceptable candidates, execute orders, and monitor portfolios for maximum performance. The tools required to successfully manage a convertible/stock hedge portfolio include research, risk-reward analysis, posture selection, and also establishing, monitoring, and closing positions.

TABLE 4-2
Alternate hedge positions in Energy Resources 9s of 1995 convertible bond, August 1980
(Investment = $1,000 per bond × 10 bonds = $10,000)

	Assumed stock price move (next 12 months)				
	−50%	−25%	0%	+25%	+50%
Stock price	7½	11¼	15	18¾	22½
Estimated bond price	78	87	100	119	140
Partial hedge: A bullish posture					
Stock sold short = 200 shares × $15 per share = $3000					
Profit or (loss) on bonds	(2200)	(1300)	0	1900	4000
Profit or (loss) on stock	1500	750	0	(750)	(1500)
Bond interest received	900	900	900	900	900
Stock dividends paid	(50)	(50)	(50)	(50)	(50)
Total profit or (loss)	150	300	850	2000	3350
Return on investment	+ 1.5%	+ 3.0%	+ 8.5%	+ 20.0%	+ 33.5%
Balanced hedge: A neutral posture					
Stock sold short = 400 shares × $15 per share = $6000					
Profit or (loss) on bonds	(2200)	(1300)	0	1900	4000
Profit or (loss) on stock	3000	1500	0	(1500)	(3000)
Bond interest received	900	900	900	900	900
Stock dividends paid	(100)	(100)	(100)	(100)	(100)
Total profit or (loss)	1600	1000	800	1200	1800
Return on investment	+ 16.0%	+ 10.0%	+ 8.0%	+ 12.0%	+ 18.0%

TABLE 4-2 *(continued)*

	Assumed stock price move (next 12 months)				
	−50%	−25%	0%	+25%	+50%
Full hedge: A bearish posture Stock sold short = 600 shares X $15 per share = $9000					
Profit or (loss) on bonds	(2200)	(1400)	0	1900	4000
Profit or (loss) on stocks	4500	2250	0	(2250)	(4500)
Bond interest received	900	900	900	900	900
Stock dividends paid	(150)	(150)	(150)	(150)	(150)
Total profit or (loss)	3050	1700	750	400	250
Return on investment	+ 30.5%	+ 17.0%	+ 7.5%	+ 4.0%	+ 2.5%

Note: Brokerage commissions were excluded from these examples for ease of illustration, but they must be considered before entering a position because they will reduce profits or increase losses.

EXHIBIT 4-2
Profit profile for Energy Resources convertible/stock hedge
(from Table 4-2)

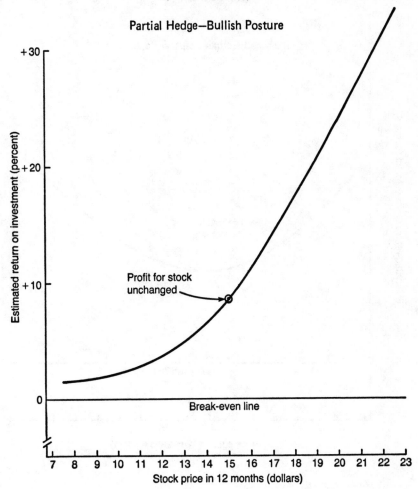

Partial Hedge—Bullish Posture

EXHIBIT 4-3
Profit profile for Energy Resources convertible/stock hedge
(from Table 4-2)

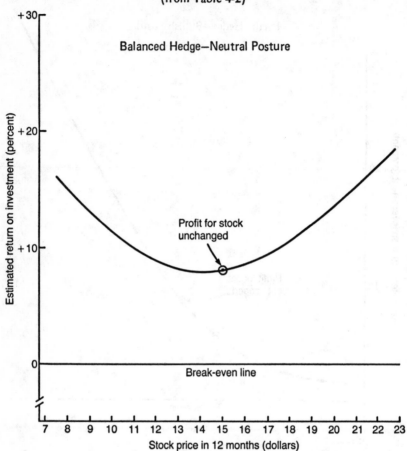

EXHIBIT 4-4
Profit profile for Energy Resources convertible/stock hedge
(from Table 4-2)

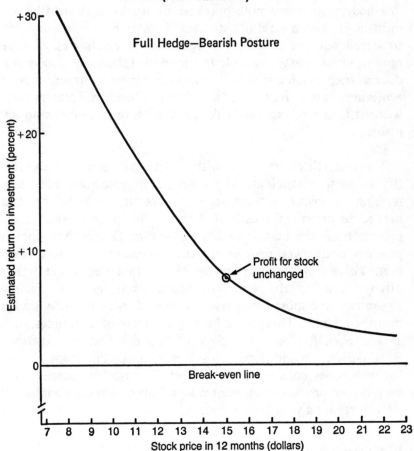

Full Hedge—Bearish Posture

Profit for stock
unchanged

Break-even line

Estimated return on investment (percent)

Stock price in 12 months (dollars)

Research

Any successful investment program, whether it involves convertible hedging or the simple purchase of stocks or straight bonds, must begin with a carefully structured research program designed to search out and identify the best possible candidates. *Average* opportunities always available in the marketplace will always produce average results. If we are to meet our investment objective of achieving a rate of return well above that offered by Treasury bills, without incurring excessive risk, our choices must be meticulously made.

The research effort begins with a systematic screening to identify all possible candidates. This can best be accomplished by subscribing to investment advisory services that provide the data needed to prepare the estimated convertible price curves. At the present time, the best service is *Value Line Convertibles* since it provides both investment values and risk-reward estimates. However, *Value Line* excludes many of the more aggressive bonds often found on the American Stock Exchange (e.g., Energy Resources) and most newly issued convertibles temporarily traded over-the-counter. These must be dug out from other sources, such as *The R.H.M. Convertible Survey*[1] and the *Standard & Poor's Bond Guide*,[2] in addition to closely monitoring the financial press for new issues coming to the market. These other sources, however, do not provide investment values. This requires the additional job of preparing your own estimates.

Risk-reward analysis

The term *risk-reward analysis* is widely misused throughout the investment community. For example, someone might think a particular stock will advance by, say, 20 percent, over the near-term but has a downside risk of only 10 percent. This gives it a supposed advantage of 2 to 1 over other stocks that presumably do not offer these favorable characteristics. By my definition of risk-reward

---

[1] Available from R.H.M. Associates, Inc., 417 Northern Blvd., Great Neck, N.Y. 11021.

[2] Available from Standard & Poor's Corporation, Publishers, 25 Broadway, New York, N.Y. 10004.

analysis, that's just someone's opinion (or guess) and should be viewed with skepticism.

Risk-reward analysis (as it pertains to convertible securities) is a mathematical evaluation of a convertible (or convertible hedge) relative to its underlying common stock, used to identify superior investment *alternatives*. While one may ultimately reject an attractive convertible opportunity because of a negative opinion on its related stock, no one's opinion on the stock plays any role in the risk-reward calculations. For example, the risk-reward anlaysis of the Energy Resources convertible bond hedge assumed only that the common stock's price would fluctuate in the future. The analysis made no attempt to forecast the price *direction*.

Risk-reward analysis is an absolute *must* when selecting convertible/stock hedges. All factors must be considered, including income received, dividends paid on stock sold short, and brokerage commissions. Not only is the analysis essential for choosing the best positions, but it will help determine target prices for future close-out.

If a position is rejected but its characteristics almost measure up to acceptable standards, don't discard your worksheet. Monitor both stock and convertible for a few weeks because their related prices may become more favorably positioned. This is especially applicable to new convertibles.

Selecting the best hedge posture

Table 4-2 presented alternate hedge positions in Energy Resources ranging from bullish to bearish investment postures. The

	Assumed stock price moves		
	−50%	0%	+50%
Partial hedge (bullish)	+ 1.5%	+8.5%	+33.5%
Balanced hedge (neutral)	+16.0%	+8.0%	+18.0%
Full hedge (bearish)	+30.5%	+7.5%	+ 2.5%

12-month profit or loss figures from Table 4-2 are repeated below for reference. As shown, the partial hedge provides about the same profit potential for a 50 percent advance (33.5 percent) as does the bearish hedge for a 50 percent decline (30.5 percent). The neutral hedge falls between the others as expected.

The odds favor a stock advancing by 50 percent more often than it declines by that amount (remember that equal probabilities are roughly −50 percent versus +100 percent). Also, we are working with low-dividend stocks and the market provides them with a greater upward price bias than it does to higher-yielding stocks. This occurs because the market's pricing mechanism takes future capital appreciation into account. Beta figures, for example, include dividends. Thus if two stocks have the same beta rating, the lower-yielding stock offers greater future *price* appreciation. For these reasons, I favor the bullish hedge—with one exception.

If the company is a likely bankruptcy candidate and its bond's current yield alone is competitive with money market instruments, a neutral or full bear hedge would be my choice. A classic example of this situation existed in early 1975 with the Pan American World Airways 7½s of 1998. At stock and bond prices of $2 and 30, respectively, the bonds were trading near their conversion value of 29 and provided a current yield of 25 percent. The neutral hedges my clients put on at the time not only locked in the 25 percent yield but produced capital gains when the company avoided bankruptcy.

Neutral or bearish hedges should be considered by investors having a bearish market outlook. Convertible hedging is an excellent strategy for market timing proponents. Technicians can quickly shift from a bullish to a bearish posture, or vice versa, by adjusting the number of shares sold short. It is not necessary for them to liquidate their entire portfolios and thereby incur heavy commission expenses; or to terminate the holding period of their securities, forcing them to accept short-term capital gains instead of favored long-term gains.

Long-term-oriented investors who do not employ market timing also may consider full bear hedges to balance unhedged convertibles in their portfolios. Assuming a well-diversified portfolio, the net result would approximate an overall low-risk posture as if each convertible security were individually hedged.

Establishing hedge positions

Research, risk-reward analysis, and hedge posture selection complete the first phase of the convertible hedge program. It is now time to execute the strategy in the dog-eat-dog atmosphere of the New York or the American Stock Exchange.

National security exchanges are a vital ingredient of viable markets. But don't for one instant believe that the specialists responsible for making orderly markets on the exchanges are there to protect your interests. Working within the framework of their own self-imposed rules and regulations, the specialists concern themselves only with maximizing profits on their time and capital invested.

As a money manager, I know there is a never-ending struggle between me and the specialists. I want the best possible prices, but so do the specialists, since they are trading for their own accounts. Their advantage comes from knowing the depth of the near-term market through open orders on their books; it is a *major* advantage. My strengths include a longer-range perspective and the ability to occasionally step ahead of them by using carefully placed limit orders. Therefore, an important requirement for successful hedging is working with a stockbroker skilled in executing highly specialized orders. Order execution skills are essential for a successful hedge program.

Consider, for example, the two-sided convertible/stock hedge, involving the purchase of bonds and the short sale of stock. First, there are price targets for the two securities. If you selected prices for your risk-reward analysis that were not representative of the market (closing prices are often not), you will not be able to execute the order. You will have to adjust your targets for realistic prices or back away from the position to await better prices. A skilled broker can help determine representative prices.

Assuming you gave your broker realistic prices based on recent trading patterns, the task is still far from over. The *listed* bond market accounts for only a small portion of the total bond trading markets. Unlike orders for listed common stocks, which must be directed to the floor of the exchange by member brokerage firms, only bond orders for nine or less must be entered on the exchange. Orders for 10 bonds or more may be executed away from the exchange (and usually are if they are active traders). Member firms attempt to keep prices on the exchange in line with off-the-board prices, but that is not always accomplished. For instance, I once received a sale price five points ($50) above the exchange-reported yearly high on a large order of convertible bonds executed in the over-the-counter market. And at times, I have willingly paid more for bonds bought off-the-board than the last traded price on the exchange.

For the uninitiated, shorting stock can be a unique experience. The main problem is the up-tick rule: Stock may be sold short only at a price that is higher than the previous price. If the common has been trading back and forth between 10 and $10\frac{1}{8}$, for example, you may sell short at $10\frac{1}{8}$ but not at 10.

The up-tick rule causes uncertainties when entering a hedge position. If the bond purchase is executed first, there is no assurance you can short the stock at a favorable price even if you enter a market order. The stock can begin declining and the first up-tick could occur at a price well below your target. Should the short side of the hedge be executed first, a market rally could force you to pay a higher price than anticipated for the bonds.

Skilled order execution by your stockbroker is mandatory for a successful hedge program. In addition to maintaining a good "feel" for both markets, based on continual monitoring of the related securities' prices, your broker should "strategize" the order. Choices to be made include whether to enter the long or short side first, whether to use market or limit orders, and then how to execute the other side once the first order is filled. In addition, your broker should evaluate the risk of starting a hedge position late in the trading day (and having the overnight risk of a one-sided position). He or she may also split up large orders into smaller units to mitigate the potential damage caused by poor prices that may be received during rapidly changing markets.

Sometimes, due to extraordinary circumstances, such as a quick rally or decline in the stock price, filling both sides of a hedge order near your target prices may not be possible. That is one of the risks you must accept when implementing a convertible hedging program. From my experience, these aberrations should work to your advantage about as often as they produce unfavorable results. If you find that on balance your luck is bad, consider finding another stockbroker.

Monitoring the hedge portfolio

Once the convertible hedge portfolio is established, hedgers may sit back and wait for major price moves before closing any positions. Or, they may actively monitor their portfolios for profit opportunities. My experience indicates that aggressive management of a hedge portfolio improves overall net investment performance, in spite of the higher brokerage commissions paid. Aggressive management also will tend to smooth out performance results from year to year. Suggested management tactics for a bullish hedge posture include the following:

1. Close out a position for profit if the convertible loses its risk-reward advantage, even if the underlying common stock has not changed much. There will probably be better hedge opportunities available at that time for reinvesting the funds.
2. Be prepared to close out positions in declining markets even if the close-out results in a modest loss. The funds might be more efficiently employed in another position that meets your purchase parameters (compared to the old hedge, which will probably just return to its starting point during the next market advance). When a stock has declined significantly, closing a position with little or no loss means that the convertible hedge has done its job. I am almost as pleased as if I were taking a profit after a rally.
3. When your investment objective is to attain relatively consistent year-to-year profits, plan to do some trading against the bonds. This will involve shorting more stock during market rallies and covering these extra shorts on market dips. These occasional adjustments will produce greater profits during broad sideways market swings at the expense of reduced prof-

its should the stock make a straight-up advance to your target close-out price.

Trading the short side

Since I advocate and practice striving to attain relatively consistent profits, the previously discussed Energy Resources bond will illustrate the pros and cons of adjusting the short side of a convertible hedge. In August 1980, I established a bullish hedge position: long 30 bonds at 100 and short 600 common at $15 (the partial hedge illustrated by Table 4-2). My target close-out was a stock price of $25. By November, the stock had advanced to nearly $24, but subsequently declined to the original $15 area in February 1981. It then rallied to $17.50 in March. If I had not adjusted the hedge by shorting more stock into rallies and covering these additional shorts on market pullbacks, the profit earned during the seven-month period would have been 9.1 percent (4.3 percent net income plus 4.8 percent appreciation). The actual trades, shown in Table 4-3, increased the total seven-month return on investment from 9.1 percent to 17.3 percent. If the stock had continued advancing to my close-out target of $25, instead of pulling back, adding to the short side during the advance would have reduced overall performance. I willingly accepted this trade-off in order to meet my objective: achieving relatively consistent returns from year-to-year.

TABLE 4-3
Short trades executed against the Energy Resources convertible bond

Additional shares sold	Date sold	Selling price	Date covered	Purchase price	Trading profits*
300 ...	11-07-80	$17.375	3-23-81	$15.125	$ 436
300 ...	11-21-80	19.50	12-15-80	17.00	496
300 ...	11-26-80	23.00	12-08-80	19.00	924
300 ...	12-23-80	19.875	1-06-81	17.00	606
300 ...	3-26-81	17.50	—	—	—
Total trading profits...					$2,462

*Trading profits are net after roundtrip brokerage commissions.

I do not employ any formal technical analysis when making investment decisions. I do utilize a "feel" for the market or the individual stock since I watch both continually (if you care to, term it *technical analysis*). Market technicians have suggested that I might be able to improve my performance by employing sophisticated market timing tools. They may be right, but I believe my time is best spent researching new convertible opportunities and managing my clients' portfolios. Technical analysis, for some, can be fun, but it can be very time-consuming. And certain technical systems would actually defeat the purpose of conservative convertible hedging. They would have you buying on upside price "breakouts," a time I would rather use to protect my paper profits by shorting into the rally. Other systems might have you trading too frequently, enriching your broker's bank account but not yours.

Closing out hedge positions

Closing a hedge position involves the same factors considered when opening a position, except that one is no longer burdened with the up-tick rule. Both sides may be closed immediately with market orders if desired. If the hedge position reaches its close-out target as a result of a major price advance within the first year, it might be desirable to hold out for long-term capital gains. In fact, convertible hedging can offer significant income tax advantages to individual investors. Assuming that profits are taken after a 12-month holding period, the profit from the long side of the position is treated as a long-term capital gain. However, the loss from the short side is always treated as a *short-term capital loss*, even though the short sale was held for over 12 months. This loss can offset short-term gains earned during the year from other hedge positions or from any other investment.

Another consideration is *how* the hedge position should be closed out after a price advance. One could, of course, sell the convertible and purchase stock to cover the short sales. However, if the convertible bond were trading at conversion value, as would be expected after a major advance, it might be better to bring the short side up to a full hedge, convert the bonds into stock, then offset the short position. This maneuver would reduce close-out brokerage commissions. It might also be a necessary tactic for capturing the bond's full conversion value if poor liquidity resulted in a bid price below conversion value. Before making a final decision, Appendix F following this chapter should be studied carefully because there are other factors to evaluate for maximum aftertax profits.

Actual hedging experience

My hedging experience encompasses a variety of market conditions, including the bear markets of 1969-70 and 1973-74 (the latter being the worst since the early 30s). In my book *How the Experts Beat the Market*, I documented the performance of convertible/stock hedges from mid-1973 to the end of 1975. (Table 4-4 highlights material from that book.) These hedges were offered to clients who managed their own accounts.

TABLE 4-4
Convertible bond/stock hedges, June 1973 through 1975,
(from *How the Experts Beat the Market*, page 37)

Convertible hedge	Date recommended	Date closed	Months	Profit or loss
Gulf Resources and Chemicals . . .	6-26-73	2-15-74	7.5	+20%
National General	6-26-73	2-15-74	7.5	+ 8
Zapata Corporation	6-26-73	12-03-74	17.0	+ 7
LTV Corp.	6-26-73	2-12-75	19.5	+21
Occidental Petroleum	6-26-73	6-16-75	23.5	+15
General Host	6-26-73	12-31-75	30.0	+39
United National	6-26-73	12-31-75	30.0	+ 1
Pan American	2-16-74	12-31-75	22.5	+26
Gulf Resources and Chemicals . . .	5-15-74	3-26-75	10.5	+ 4
Brown Company	8-12-74	11-11-74	3.0	+ 9
Gould Incorporated	8-12-74	12-03-74	17.0	+14
Fibreboard	10-01-74	3-26-75	6.0	+ 9
Republic N.Y.	10-01-74	11-11-74	1.5	+ 8
Northwest Industries	1-02-75	2-12-75	1.5	+14
Averages (14 positions)			14 Mo.	+14%

Note: These hedges were recommended by the author for an investment advisory service. Each hedge was designed for profits during bull markets, at limited downside risk, without attempting to predict future price trends. If a hedge position was proposed more than once (or if a similar hedge position in the same company was suggested) while the initial recommendation was still rated a buy or hold, only the initial recommendation is shown. Profit or loss figures are based on nonleveraged positions, and all commission expenses, dividends paid, and bond interest received are included.

As demonstrated by Table 4-4, all hedge positions were profitable in spite of going through the worst bear market in over 40 years. At no time during this stock market crash were convertible hedge positions down more than 5 percent on average, despite the "investment floors'" plunge as interest rates rose to then-historic highs. Over the full two and one half-year period, the average profit of 14 percent for 14 months (Table 4-4) produced an average annual return of 12 percent; well above the 7 percent earned from Treasury bills during that same time.

Actual performance for the 27 different positions closed out over the six-year period, commencing in late 1975 through December 31, 1981, are presented in Table 4-5. Of the 27 positions, 25 showed a profit and 2 were closed at a loss. The average profit of 10.7 percent for 7.9 months produced an average annual rate of return of 16.3 percent. This far surpassed the average return of less than 9 percent available from Treasury bills over that period.

When I wrote this chapter in mid-1981, Treasury bill yields were advancing toward their 1980 record high of 18 percent and the stock market had drifted by more than 15 percent from its bull market high reached in November 1980. The question asked more and more frequently was, "Why assume the extra risk of convertible hedging when historically high yields are available from risk-free money market instruments?" Even hedging professionals had indicated they were shifting funds into Treasury bills or other short-term paper. This was a difficult and important question, which justifiably concerns conservative investors.

My answer was twofold. First, short-term interest rate peaks are not representative of what can be expected over a longer time frame. For instance, Treasury bills reached 15 percent in early 1980, declined to under 7 percent by summer, then rose to 18 percent later in the year. They wound up with an 11.4 percent *average* rate of return for the entire year. Another comparison, money market funds, investing in higher risk commercial paper and bank certificates, paid about 12 percent for the year.

Second, the stock market has been very sensitive to interest rate trends in recent years. Interest rate peaks have closely coincided with stock market bottoms. As a result, switching from equities to

TABLE 4-5

Convertible bond/stock hedges, 1976 through 1981

Company	Bond description	Opened	Closed	Months held	Net total return
Pan American	7.50 -98	12-31-75	6-17-76	5.6	+ 7.1%
Avco Corp.	9.625-01	10-07-76	12-02-76	1.8	+ 4.0
Pan American	7.50 -98	10-29-76	3-24-77	4.8	+ 3.9
Harrah's	7.50 -96	6-21-77	5-16-78	10.8	+14.9
Avco Corp.	9.625-01	6-21-77	7-21-78	13.0	+18.4
Pan American	7.50 -98	6-21-77	9-01-78	15.3	+15.9
Grumman	8.00 -99	7-28-77	5-09-78	9.4	+ 3.5
Cooper Laboratories	4.50 -92	12-30-77	12-09-80	35.3	+17.3
Allegheny Airlines	9.25 -99	5-09-78	6-23-78	1.5	+10.1
Phoenix Steel	6.00 -87	6-05-78	3-30-79	9.8	−11.5
TRE Corp.	9.75 -02	6-10-78	9-15-78	3.2	+ 2.7
General Instrument	10.25 -96	6-15-78	8-14-78	2.0	+ 4.4
Eastern Airlines	10.00 -02	6-26-78	8-20-78	1.8	+ 1.6
Mohawk Data Sciences	12.00 -89	7-17-78	9-14-78	1.9	− 7.6
Ramada Inns	10.00 -00	8-17-78	5-02-79	8.5	+43.4
NFC Corp.	8.00 -92	10-02-79	11-15-80	13.5	+19.3
Phoenix Steel	6.00 -87	1-10-80	5-29-80	4.6	+ 5.2
Instrument Systems	12.00 -99	2-19-80	9-02-80	18.4	+17.5
Ramada Inns	10.00 -00	4-28-80	5-08-81	12.2	+21.7
Ozark Airlines	5.25 -86	5-23-80	4-10-81	10.5	+23.7
Tyco Laboratories	5.875-88	6-01-80	8-15-80	2.5	+13.2

LTV Corp.	12.00 -05	6-02-80	11-10-80	5.3	+ 8.8
Vernitron	5.75 -82	9-02-80	11-15-80	2.5	+14.8
U.S. Realty Investment	5.75 -89	9-15-80	5-01-81	7.5	+ 9.5
Sanders Associates	7.00 -92	10-14-80	2-18-81	4.1	+ 3.0
Aeroflex Laboratories	10.00 -99	12-03-80	6-01-81	5.9	+15.6
Oak Industries	11.00 -00	9-23-81	10-30-81	1.2	+ 7.9
Averages (27 positions)				7.9 Mo.	+10.7%

Note: This table presents listed convertible bond/stock hedge positions taken for the author's first major managed account from late 1975 (partial positions below $15,000 in size were excluded). Beginning in 1980, the results are shown for the first client entering the position. Actual results were adjusted to reflect the higher full-service brokerage commissions prevailing in 1981. Positions still open on 12/31/81 were excluded. These open positions were producing profits at a rate comparable to the ones closed out.

Treasury bills is likely to take place at stock market lows, and switching back to equities after stocks have rallied is obviously a losing proposition. One pension fund client, for example (managed by an investment adviser who executes orders through my firm) shifted funds from their convertible securities account to six-month bank certificates of deposit three times over the past two years (against the adviser's wishes). Their market timing appeared to be near faultless because yields received ranged up to almost 20 percent. However, without exception, the managed convertible securities portfolio outperformed the certificates for each six-month period, despite the convertible account having to incur the additional commission expenses of liquidating positions and reinvesting the funds when they returned: In addition, the fund trustees spend valuable time watching the money markets and shopping for the best rate of interest.

Our capital markets respond rather quickly to changing conditions. As illustrated by the capital market line in the Introduction, the markets will not allow investors to receive a greater return from risk-free instruments than that available from higher-risk strategies over the long term. The markets are too efficient to allow it. As an example, convertible bonds employed in my hedging strategies today not only carry coupons far larger than those of a few years back, they are also trading at lower conversion premiums. This is the market's way of assuring higher gains in the future. Your time is better spent researching new hedge positions, and managing your portfolio, than in watching interest rate cycles. Convertible hedging is a superior strategy for the long term, and the short term should not be a major concern. The small amount of extra near-term risk is well worth taking.

Hedging on margin

For those investors who can accept somewhat higher risk, or are in relatively high income tax brackets, convertible hedges can be margined. Not only should the use of margin improve pretax performance, it offers substantial tax advantages.

Table 4-6 presents the partial hedge for Energy Resources (Table 4-2) based on the margin requirement at the time of 50

TABLE 4-6
A partial hedge position in Energy Resources 9s of 1995 on margin,
August 1980

Position

10 bonds long versus 200 shares of stock sold short
Net investment = 10 bonds X $1,000 per bond X 50 percent margin = $5,000
Funds borrowed from brokerage firm at 14 percent interest = $5,000

Risk-reward analysis

	Assumed stock price move (next 12 months)		
	−50%	0%	+50%
Stock price	7½	15	22½
Estimated bond price	78	100	140
Profit or (loss) on bonds	(2200)	0	4000
Profit or (loss) on stock	1500	0	(1500)
Bond interest received	900	900	900
Stock dividends paid	(50)	(50)	(50)
Margin interest paid	(700)	(700)	(700)
Total profit or (loss)	(550)	150	2650
Return on investment	− 11.0%	+ 3.0%	+ 53.0%
Return on investment for nonmargined hedge position from Table 4-2	+ 1.5%	+ 8.5%	+ 33.5%

Note: Brokerage commissions were excluded from this example for ease of illustration, but they must be considered before entering a position because they will reduce profits or increase losses.

percent for convertible bonds. Margin interest charged by the brokerage firm was assumed to be 14 percent. Although it has varied considerably above and below that rate in recent years, 14 percent represents a realistic average.

As shown by Table 4-6, the use of margin increases the profit potential (53.0 percent versus 33.5 percent) while also increasing risk (−11.0 percent versus +1.5 percent). Margin can increase the expected rate of return over the long term, provided that hedge positions perform better than the rate of margin interest charged. However, the most important benefits to be gained from employing margin are the tax advantages for investors in high federal income tax brackets.

Table 4-7 compares the margined position from Table 4-6 with the nonmargined position for aftertax performance. For a 50 percent stock advance, the aftertax return on margin is about 17 percentage points higher (41.5 percent versus 24.2 percent). For a 50 percent decline the disadvantage is only about 8 percentage points

TABLE 4-7
Comparison of aftertax performance for margined and nonmargined hedge positions in Energy Resources, August 1980

Assumptions

1. All capital gains or losses are taxed as long-term (short-term gains or losses are offset by other transactions).
2. The investor is in the 50 percent federal income tax bracket (20 percent for long-term capital gains).

Aftertax risk-reward analysis

	Assumed stock price move (next 12 months)		
	−50%	0%	+50%
Nonmargined position:			
Investment = $10,000			
Capital gain or (loss)	(700)	0	2500
Taxes (paid) or saved	140	0	(500)
Net income received	850	850	850
Taxes (paid)	(425)	(425)	(425)
Net aftertax profit or (loss)	(135)	425	2425
Aftertax return on investment	− 1.4%	+ 4.2%	+ 24.2%
Margined position:			
Investment = $5,000			
Capital gain or (loss)	(700)	0	2500
Taxes (paid) or saved	140	0	(500)
Net income received	150	150	150
Taxes (paid)	(75)	(75)	(75)
Net aftertax profit or (loss)	(485)	75	2075
Aftertax return on investment	− 9.7%	+ 1.5%	+ 41.5%

(−9.7 percent versus −1.4 percent). (Remember, stocks are more likely to advance by 50 percent than they are to decline by that amount.)

Margined convertible/stock hedges may be employed as a separate investment strategy or be treated as additions to portfolios of unhedged convertibles on high-quality common stocks. Considering the higher volatility of the underlying hedged stocks (compared to unhedged higher-quality securities) the hedges would be expected to outperform the unhedged convertibles in rising markets at about the same level of risk.

APPENDIX E

Selling stock short

To sell stock short is to sell stock that one does not own. The shares are borrowed by the broker from another customer of the firm who holds them in a margin account, from another brokerage firm, or from an institutional lender. At some future time, investors must cover their short sales by buying the same amount of securities originally sold short and returning them to the lender.

The up-tick rule

With but few technical exceptions, securities may be sold short only on an "up-tick" or a "zero-plus tick" (the last change in the security's price must have been an increase). This regulation was designed to prevent speculators from driving down the price of a security by uncontrolled short selling.

Short-exempt sales

The up-tick rule does not apply when securities are sold on a short-exempt basis. To qualify a short sale as exempt, sellers must give their brokers irrevocable instructions to convert their bonds or preferreds and to deliver the stock received upon conversion to cover the short sale.

Margin rules

Short sales may be made only in a margin account. Cash or marginable collateral must be deposited against the short sale in accordance with applicable margin regulations (currently 50 percent). No additional collateral is required if the short sale is made against convertible securities, providing they are exchangeable within 90 days (some delayed convertibles would not qualify). This exception recognizes the safety of a short sale made against a convertible security.

Funds received from the short sale

The funds from a short sale are credited to the short account and are held by the brokerage firm (or forwarded to the lender of the securities if the brokerage firm cannot obtain the securities from another client of the firm). The resulting credit balance, therefore, is "frozen" from use by the short seller. The brokerage firm or other lender gets the use of the funds.

Marking to the market

Once a short sale has been executed and the price of the security changes, the brokerage firm will adjust the balance (in the short account) which resulted from the sale so that the amount needed for repurchase is held. This process is called "marking to the market" and simply involves offsetting debit and credit entries between the short account and the regular margin account. If the securities sold short decline in price, the short account is debited and an offsetting credit entry is made in the general margin account. Should the securities rise in price, the margin account is debited and the short account credited. The credit balance in the short account will then again equal the current market value of the securities sold short. Note that a hedge account might begin with no debit balance in its general margin account but, as a result of debit entries during a rising market, margin interest would be charged on the resultant debit balance.

Cash dividends

Since a short sale creates more owners than is shown on the company's books, short sellers must pay any cash dividends that are declared by the company. For this reason, securities which do not pay high dividends are generally preferred by short sellers to minimize the cost of the dividends.

Stock splits

The number of shares held short in the account is automatically adjusted by the brokerage firm to reflect stock splits or dividends paid in additional shares. In a 3-for-2 split, for example, 200 shares held short increases to 300.

Short squeezes

When excessive short selling takes place in a particular security and it becomes difficult or impossible to borrow the security, a temporary shortage of stock for borrowing may exist. For instance, the lender may sell the shares himself, making them no longer available to the borrower, who must relinquish the short position by purchase. The rush to cover by the "squeezed" short sellers may force prices up sharply. A shortage will usually develop if a tender offer is made for the common stock.

APPENDIX F

Closing a convertible position
via the conversion process

The limited liquidity for convertible securities works to the investor's advantage since institutional money managers are forced to use the larger markets in stocks and straight bonds. This helps to create undervalued opportunities like those illustrated in Chapters 3 and 4, but it also means that at times for some convertibles a necessary order execution at a fair price may simply be impossible. There are ways to deal with this problem.

Convertible positions are usually closed out after a significant price advance, at which time the convertible is no longer an attractive alternative to its common stock. However, if the convertible is not actively traded, the best bid may be below its conversion value. Rather than sell at a discount, the preferred method for closing the position often will be to exchange the convertible for common stock and sell the more actively traded common. In actual practice, the common stock usually is sold short first, and the stock received later via the conversion process is used to offset the short sale.

When considering close out via the conversion process, here are the major factors to consider:

1. Accrued interest is lost when a bond is converted.
2. The capital to carry the position during the conversion period (about four weeks) will not be earning any return (90 percent

may be released for other investments, but margin interest will be charged on the resulting debit balance).
3. Dividends must be paid if the shorted stock declares a dividend during the conversion period and the record date falls within that conversion period.
4. Brokerage commissions will be different and should be taken into account.

To illustrate these points, consider a convertible/stock hedge in the Energy Resources 9s of 1995 bond of Chapter 4. Assume the common stock had risen to $25 per share on May 1, 1981, and a position of long 10 bonds (equal to 615 shares) versus 400 shares short was to be closed out. At $25, the bond's conversion value was $153¾ ($25 X 61.5 shares = $1,537.50) but the best bid was only 150. The bond pays its semiannual interest on June 1 ($45 for each bond) and the common stock goes ex-dividend on May 6 ($.06 per share due, since the short position is held through the May 13 stock of record date).

Three possible courses of action would be considered: immediate close-out, short 215 additional shares and convert immediately, or short 215 additional shares and convert after the June 1 interest date. The arithmetic for evaluating these alternatives is shown in Table F-1.

From this analysis, the normal choice would be to convert after June 1. The additional $513 earned ($15,688 − $15,175) on the $15,000 position for less than two additional months equates to an annualized rate of return above 20 percent.

For investors in high income tax brackets it may be more advantageous to execute the immediate close-out strategy. If the position were held over 12 months, the profits earned from the bonds held long would be treated as long-term capital gains. The losses on the shorted stock would be short-term. If the position were closed out by conversion, a portion of the bonds would be treated as if they were sold the day open short sale positions were executed (possibly the same day). The balance would be treated as being held long-term. Rather than accept an abnormally low bid from the exchange, ask your broker if the firm's arbitrage

TABLE F-1
Alternate methods for closing a convertible hedge position

Immediate close out

Sell 10 bonds at 150	=	$ 15,000
Accrued bond interest for five months	=	375
Cover 400 common at $25	=	(10,000)
Commissions	=	(200)
Release of funds held in short account	=	10,000
Net proceeds on settlement date in one week	=	$ 15,175

Go to full hedge and immediately convert

Short 215 common at $25	=	$ 5,375
Commissions	=	(120)
Release of funds held on short account	=	10,000
Net proceeds upon receipt of shares from conversion in about one month	=	$ 15,255

Go to full hedge and convert after June 1

Short 215 common at $25	=	$ 5,375
Commissions	=	(120)
Interest received for six months	=	450
Dividends paid = 615 shares X $.06	=	(37)
Release of funds held in short account	=	10,000
Net proceeds upon receipt of shares from conversion in about two months	=	$ 15,688

department would be willing to take the entire position into its inventory at more favorable prices. This question should probably be asked before opening an account since it is a close-out strategy that you will wish to employ frequently. My firm's policy, for example, is to purchase the bonds only at a discount that reflects the cost of money during the conversion process (usually about four weeks) and the accrued bond interest lost (if any).

Note that when short positions are traded over the life of a hedge position, the investor may specify which short sale is being covered for tax planning purposes.

CHAPTER 5

Hedging convertibles with put and call options

In this chapter, while hedging concepts are still fresh in your mind, we will proceed directly to the use of puts and calls with convertibles. My intention is not to emphasize options, but to explain their use as a *tool* within the context of convertible hedging strategies.

Readers not familiar with listed options can have their stockbroker provide informative booklets and the prospectus issued by the option exchanges. Libraries should also have several basic books on the subject for your further study. Appendix G, immediately following this chapter, provides examples of the more popular put and call strategies and should be studied before proceeding. This is all *must reading* if you are not knowledgeable in the option field.

When not to use puts and calls

There is probably no other area of the securities markets as misunderstood, or as abused, as listed options. Numerous strategies have been touted as offering investors extra profits from their investment capital. The most popular has been the sale of covered calls against common stocks. Call writers (sellers) hope to earn extra profits from the premiums received. However, while the strategy's risk is lower than owning stocks unhedged, potential losses are reduced only by the premiums. In bull markets the calls will be exercised, thus taking away any opportunity for large capital gains (see basic option strategy 3 of Appendix G).

Since listed options first began trading in 1973, many financial writers have used so-called track records and hypothetical studies to support claims of desirability for continuous option-writing programs. Others, myself included, have argued that covered call writing is doomed to failure because of many factors, not the least of which is the high trading expenses incurred with the strategy.

Although some may say "The jury is still out," I believe the past eight years provide sufficient proof that the strategy doesn't work. As an example, there are five major call option-selling mutual funds, which have been in operation for the last four years, each with the promising term *income* in its name. Their actual investment results are presented in Table 5-1, covering the period from inception in mid-1977 to mid-1981. As evinced by the table, the average annual rate of return of 7.1 percent is far below that promised when the funds were first marketed to the public; it is even below the return of risk-free money market instruments (Treasury bills averaged nearly 10 percent for the four years). It is important to note that these poor results were achieved during a market environment conducive to maximum performance by option-writing programs—*rising stock prices and rising option premiums*. These results explain why new option-selling funds have not been brought to the market since 1977 and why most of the original five have experienced net redemptions in recent years. We are now seeing articles in the financial press taking a cold, hard look at the strategy.

Other available option strategies are not any better (some are worse) than covered call writing when employed on a continuous basis. The option market has become efficient, and neither the seller nor the buyer can gain an ongoing advantage over the other. The only consistent winners are the stockbrokers who collect commissions from both sides of each trade.

TABLE 5-1
Results of a group of option-selling mutual funds over a four-year period
through June 1981

Starting date	Fund	Original issue price*	Net asset value†	Cash distri- butions	Adjusted net asset value‡	Total return§
4/77	... Colonial Option Income	$12.50	$10.58	$5.54	$16.12	29.0%
6/77	... Federated Option Income	15.00	12.52	4.84	17.36	15.7
6/77	... Kemper Option Income	15.00	13.65	6.31	19.96	33.1
10/77	... Oppenheimer Option Income	25.00	24.34	8.46	32.80	31.2
6/77	... Putnam Option Income	15.00	14.11	5.76	19.87	32.5
	Average total return					28.3%
	Average annual return					7.1%

*Includes 8.5 percent load charge.
†As of 6/30/81.
‡Net asset value plus cash distributions equals adjusted net asset value.
§On original issue price over four years.

I believe the only time options can enhance your stock port-folio is when premium levels are abnormally high or low. When premiums are too high, puts and calls might be sold, and if premi-ums are too low, options might be purchased. You should not plan on implementing any option strategy continuously since these abnormal market conditions occur infrequently (less than 10 per-cent of the time). And remember that commissions must be taken into account when considering any short-term trading vehicle; an otherwise overpriced call option may not be an attractive sale can-didate after deducting appropriate brokerage commissions from the premium received.

When to use puts and calls

Although options are far from an investment panacea, investors skilled in hedging undervalued convertibles *can* employ puts and calls, for the purpose of reducing risk, on a continuous basis. The sale of a normally valued call option, for example, would not be expected to enhance performance but rather would be expected to reduce risk, much like the short sale of common stock discussed in the last chapter. Selling calls is usually superior to shorting stock since the proceeds received from the option sale are immedi-ately available to the investor.

In addition, put options may be purchased to protect a convert-ible, or puts and calls may be combined to create a fabricated "short sale" of the common stock. Examples will be presented later in this chapter but first consider an actual hedge position which involved the sale of covered calls as a superior alternative to selling stock short.

Hedging the LTV Corporation 12s of 2005 convertible bond

My experience with the LTV convertible bond will illustrate how the sale of options can be superior to the short sale of stock as part of a hedging strategy. When faced with this choice you should perform the same calculations yourself before making a decision.

In June 1980, I established bullish hedge positions with the LTV 12s of 2005 by shorting common stock against the convertible bond similar to the partial hedge position for Energy Resources in the last chapter. Each LTV bond was exchangeable into 82.6 shares of common. For each 10 bonds purchased at 100 (equivalent to 826 shares of stock), the partial hedge involved 300 shares of common sold short at $10.75. Listed put or call options were not available on LTV Corporation at that time.

Soon after I established the convertible/stock hedge position, the common began to rise so I added to the short side of the hedge. By November, the stock had advanced to $16 and the short side had been increased from 300 shares to 600 shares for each 10 bonds. As shown by the convertible price curve of Exhibit 5-1, the bond was trading at 135 with the stock at $16. My close-out target was stock and bond prices of about $18 and 150 respectively.

In November, the American Stock Exchange introduced listed put and call options on LTV. This produced various new alternatives to consider. The choice quickly narrowed down to the sale of calls, however, as premium levels reached an abnormally high level at the time.

Table 5-2 compares the sale of call options with the short sale of common stock. Profit profiles for the two alternatives are displayed in Exhibit 5-2. Although the reason for switching from the short position to call options is obvious from the table and exhibit, please take a few moments to study the data. Major points to consider are:

1. The convertible/stock hedge required an investment of $13,500, compared to $10,300 for the convertible/call option hedge. Remember, proceeds from short selling are not available to the seller whereas call option premiums are, and may be used to reduce the cost of the position.
2. The convertible/stock hedge would not be as attractive if established at prices of $16 and 135 for the stock and bond as

EXHIBIT 5-1
The convertible price curve for LTV 12s of 2005 convertible bond,
November 1980 (conversion ratio = 82.6 shares)

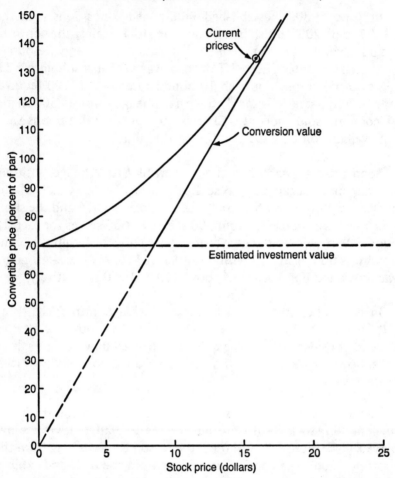

TABLE 5-2
Risk-reward analysis for alternate hedge positions in LTV 12s of 2005 convertible bond, November 1980

	LTV stock price in June 1981 (7 months)				
	10	15	16	20	25
Estimated bond price	100	128	135	166	207
June 15 call price*	0	0	1	5	10
Convertible/stock hedge					
Buy 10 bonds at 135 = $13,500					
Sell short 600 common at $16 = $ 9,600					
Investment = $13,500					
Profit or (loss) on bonds	(3500)	(700)	0	3100	7200
Profit or (loss) on stock	3600	600	0	(2400)	(5400)
Bond interest received	700	700	700	700	700
Total profit or (loss)	800	600	700	1400	2500
Percent return for 7 months	+ 5.9	+ 4.4	+ 5.2	+ 10.4	+ 18.5
Convertible/call option hedge					
Buy 10 bonds at 135 = $13,500					
Sell 8 June 15 calls at 4 = − 3,200					
Investment = $10,300					
Profit or (loss) on bonds	(3500)	(700)	0	3100	7200
Profit or (loss) on calls	3200	3200	2400	(800)	(4800)
Bond interest received	700	700	700	700	700
Total profit or (loss)	600	3200	3100	3000	3100
Percent return for 7 months	+ 5.8	+ 31.1	+ 30.1	+ 29.1	+ 30.1
Advantage for call option hedge	− 0.1	+ 26.7	+ 24.9	+ 18.7	+ 11.6

Note: Brokerage commissions to switch from stock to call options totaled about 3 percent of the $10,300 new investment requirement.
*Each call represents 100 shares of common stock (e.g., a price of 1 means $100). Prices shown are the call's intrinsic value at expiration.

EXHIBIT 5-2
Profit profiles for alternate hedge positions in LTV 12s of 2005
convertible bond (from Table 5-2)

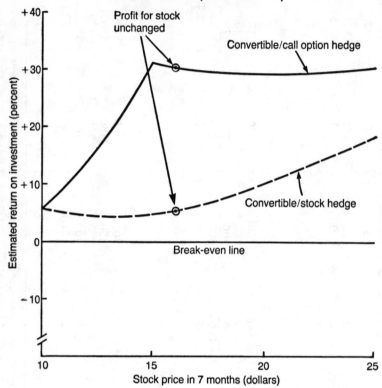

when initially established at $10.75 and 100. Most of the profit potential had already been attained as the bond neared its target close-out price of 150.

3. The convertible/call option hedge was very attractive. Option premiums had advanced to a historically high level in response to rising short-term interest rates and increased volatility of LTV's common stock.

4. The profit potential for the covered call option hedge was relatively constant at all prices above the $15 exercise price. Covered call writing provides a "cap" on profits once the stock advances to the call's exercise price.

All factors considered, the sale of call options against the LTV convertible debenture was a superior investment strategy in November 1980. The bond was modestly undervalued and option premiums were abnormally high. The convertible/call option hedge offered a potential annualized rate of return (excluding commissions) of about 50 percent (30 percent for seven months from Table 5-2) while providing downside protection against a stock price decline of about 40 percent (from $16 down to under $10).

A negative possibility was that LTV would call the bond for redemption prior to its May 15, 1981, interest payment date, forcing holders to convert into common stock. The loss of bond interest would reduce the computed annualized return to about 40 percent. The fact that the position could be closed out prior to June 1981 if the call option were to lose most of its premium over intrinsic value, offset this unfavorable contingency.[1] An early close-out had the potential of increasing the annualized return from the hedge position (e.g., 90 percent of the profit potential in three fourths the time).

Both of these possibilities actually occured. The bonds were called in early 1981. In March, the common stock received via conversion was sold $24\frac{1}{8}$ and the June 15 calls were covered (bought back) at $9\frac{1}{2}$, only $\frac{3}{8}$ over their intrinsic value of $9\frac{1}{8}$

---

[1] A call option's intrinsic value is determined by subtracting its exercise price from the current stock price. In the example, the $4 call had an intrinsic value of $1 ($16 stock price — $15 exercise price = $1). The $3 difference is termed *time value* and must vanish when the option expires.

$(24\frac{1}{8} - 15 = 9\frac{1}{8})$. The position was not worth holding for another three months (until the options expired) since only the $\frac{3}{8}$ of a point ($37.50) time value could be added to profits already accumulated ($300 for eight calls, or 3 percent for three months). An exception to the early close-out decision was the desire by some clients to hold their positions until June to establish long-term capital gains.

Convertible/option hedges in Zenith Radio

In April 1981, Zenith Radio's common stock was trading at $18 and its $8\frac{3}{8}$s of 2005 convertible debenture was at 100. From the convertible price curve of Exhibit 5-3, and the risk-reward analysis of Table 5-3, the bond was a superior investment opportunity. For stock price changes of 50 percent, the bond's stock equivalency was 48 percent and its market advantage was 1.3.

$$SE = \frac{(\text{Convertible risk}) - (\text{Bond return})}{(\text{Stock risk}) - (\text{Bond return})}$$

$$= \frac{(-15) - (-14)}{(-47) - (-14)}$$

$$= \frac{-29}{-61}$$

$$= .48$$

$$MA = \frac{(\text{Convertible return})}{.48(\text{Stock return}) + .52(\text{Bond return})}$$

$$= \frac{+43}{.48(+53) + .52(+14)}$$

$$= \frac{+43}{+25.4 + 7.3}$$

$$= \frac{+43}{32.7}$$

$$= 1.32$$

The Zenith Radio convertible was an attractive candidate for unhedged portfolios, as discussed in Chapter 3. Or it could have been hedged with listed put and call options, the choice being

EXHIBIT 5-3
The convertible price curve for Zenith Radio $8\frac{3}{8}$s of 2005 convertible
bond, April 1981 (conversion ratio = 49.1 shares)

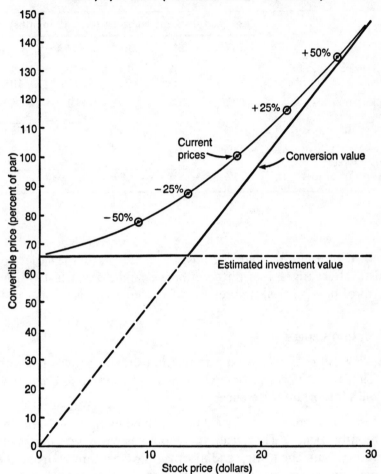

TABLE 5-3
Risk-reward analysis for Zenith Radio 8⅜s of 2005 convertible bond,
April 1981

	Assumed stock price change (next 12 months)				
	−50%	−25%	0%	+25%	+50%
Stock price	9	13½	18	22½	27
Estimated bond price ...	77	87½	100	116	135
Stock gain or loss	−50%	−25%	0%	+ 25%	+ 50%
Plus dividends	+ 3	+ 3	+ 3	+ 0	+ 3
Net profit or loss	−47%	−22%	+ 3%	+ 28%	+ 53%
Convertible gain or loss. ...	−23%	−13%	0%	+ 16%	+ 35%
Plus interest	+ 8	+ 8	+ 8	+ 8	+ 8
Net profit or loss	−15%	− 5%	+ 8%	+ 24%	+ 43%

governed by one's desired risk posture. To illustrate the variety of realistic alternatives, four different hedge candidates, selected from dozens of possibilities, are presented for your analysis.

Call option hedges

Selling call options against a convertible creates a lower-risk posture similar to the convertible/stock hedge illustrated in Chapter 4, but with important differences.

1. Listed call options are issued having fixed expiration dates nine months hence. Thus, calls may be viewed as wasting assets throughout their life, and profits may be earned from the decaying premiums without requiring the stock to advance in price.

2. A call option's premium (the call's traded price) can never be as high as the price of its underlying common stock and is usually only a small fraction of its stock's price. Thus, the short sale of common stock provides more dollars to protect the convertible against a major price decline.

3. The sale of an in-the-money call (with a higher premium) provides more protection than an out-of-the-money call, but at the same time limits potential profits of the hedge.

4. The convertible/call option hedge will perform best during

relatively stable periods in the market while convertible/stock hedges thrive on market volatility. Calls should be sold against the higher-quality, low-risk convertibles while short positions involving common stock are more appropriate for the aggressive, more speculative convertibles.

Table 5-4 presents a convertible/call option hedge in Zenith Radio. Since 10 bonds are exchangeable into 491 shares of common, the sale of four calls is defined as a *covered* position (a fifth call would technically be uncovered, or "naked"). The August 20 call was selected from among calls expiring in May, August, and November with exercise prices of $10, $15, $20, and $25. August 20 was the *middle* month call option, trading 10 percent out-of-the-money (its common stock was trading at $18).

The risk-reward analysis of Table 5-4 shows that the hedge would perform satisfactorily if the stock remained unchanged at $18 or advanced above the $20 exercise price. It would lose money at stock prices of about $15 and below. Covered call option writing is a bullish posture since one always wants the common stock to advance to the call's exercise price or above, at the time the option expires.

Note that the number of calls sold against a convertible trading at a premium over its conversion value is usually less than a fully covered position would suggest. This compensates for the loss of conversion premium upon a stock price advance. Always prepare a worksheet analysis and profit profile before selecting the precise number of calls to sell.

For investors desiring more protection, and who are willing to concede some of the potential profits, I present a neutral hedge position (ratio hedge) in Table 5-5. This hedge involves eight calls versus 10 bonds (4 calls are covered and 4 are uncovered).

The profit profiles comparing the two alternatives are shown in Exhibit 5-4. Notice that the ratio hedge provides a greater return, or less risk, at all prices below $21.50 at expiration. Its disadvantage is the possibility that Zenith's common might experience a major price advance and expose the hedge to large losses at stock

TABLE 5-4
Risk-reward analysis for Zenith Radio convertible bond combined with call options, April 1981

Hedge workout for bullish posture

Position:

Buy 10 bonds at 100   = $10,000
Sell 4 August 20 calls at 1½   =   − 600
Investment   = $ 9,400

Risk-reward analysis:

Prices at expiration					
Stock	9	15	18	20	27
Bond	77	91	100	107	135
Call	0	0	0	0	7
Profit or (loss)					
Bonds	(2300)	(900)	0	700	3500
Calls	600	600	600	600	(2200)
Bond interest for four months	280	280	280	280	280
Net profit or (loss)	(1420)	(20)	880	1580	1580
Percent return					
Four months	− 15.1	− 0.2	+ 9.4	+ 16.8	+ 16.8
Annualized	− 45.3	− 0.6	+ 28.2	+ 50.4	+ 50.4

TABLE 5-5
Risk-reward analysis for Zenith Radio convertible bond combined with call options, April 1981

Hedge workout for neutral posture

Position:

Buy 10 bonds at 100 = $10,000
Sell 8 August 20 calls at 1½ = − 1,200
Investment = $ 8,800

Risk-reward analysis:

Prices at expiration					
Stock	9	15	18	20	27
Bond	77	91	100	107	135
Call	0	0	0	0	7
Profit or (loss)					
Bonds	(2300)	(900)	0	700	3500
Calls	1200	1200	1200	1200	(4400)
Bond interest for four months	280	280	280	280	280
Net profit or (loss)	(820)	580	1480	2180	(620)
Percent return					
Four months	− 9.3	+ 6.6	+ 16.8	+ 24.8	− 7.0
Annualized	− 28.0	+ 19.8	+ 50.4	+ 74.4	− 21.0

EXHIBIT 5-4
Profit profiles for alternate convertible/call option hedge
positions in Zenith Radio (from Tables 5-4 and 5-5)

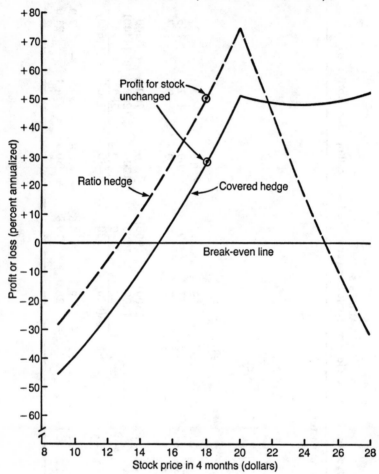

prices above its $25 upper breakeven point. Usually, one can close out a ratio hedge for profits as the stock advances above the call's exercise price, even if the call has a few months remaining life. However, in recent years, we have witnessed an increasing number of corporate acquisitions. Upon a takeover announcement, the stock's price could immediately leap to well above the upper breakeven point, depriving the hedger of any opportunity to take protective action. For this reason, I only employ ratio hedges in well-diversified portfolios and try to avoid companies that are likely takeover candidates. In addition, I will consider ratio hedges only during those infrequent periods when the *overall* level of option premiums is abnormally high. (A high premium for a specific option might indicate that the company is a takeover target.)

Which call to sell

As illustrated by the Zenith Radio example, I generally prefer the middle month and a call trading out-of-the-money. The middle month usually offers the best trade-offs among premium level, commission expense, and trading liquidity. An out-of-the-money call normally provides a sufficient premium for protecting an undervalued convertible while offering greater upside opportunity than one trading at- or in-the-money. These are my usual parameters, but market conditions sometimes force me to seek other alternatives.

Put option hedges

The purchase of put options is frequently touted as a means to protect common stocks against a price decline. The objective is to limit downside loss to the premiums paid, while providing full upside opportunity (minus the premiums, of course). The term often used is *insurance,* but is it really a prudent tactic for conservative investors? That one loses most of the premiums during sideways markets is seldom mentioned.

I do not approve of the indiscriminate purchase of put options. Since losses are virtually assured under most stock market movements (down, sideways, or modestly higher), I doubt the occasional bull market can produce sufficient profits to offset the cost of repeated "insurance" premiums, much less earn a reasonable profit. As for being prudent, the risk-reward posture is essentially the same as the speculative purchase of naked call options (see basic option strategies 2 and 2a of Appendix G following this chapter).

Having said that, I will now illustrate that put options *can* be employed effectively as part of a hedge program involving under-valued convertibles. The primary difference between buying puts to protect common stocks and buying them to protect under-valued convertibles is this: *The convertibles do not require as much protection.* They can be protected with fewer puts, thus reducing the cost of the "insurance."

This point is demonstrated by the convertible/put option hedge position for Zenith Radio in Table 5-6. Ten bonds are the equiva-lent of nearly 500 shares, but only two puts are required for pro-tective purposes. The savings in premium dollars are transferred directly to the bottom line. Exhibit 5-5 shows an attractive profit profile for the Zenith convertible/put option hedge.

Put and call option hedges combined

Puts and calls may also be used to create convertible/option hedge positions having unusual risk-reward characteristics. For example, the purchase of a put combined with the sale of a call is essentially the same thing as selling 100 shares of common stock short (see basic option strategies 6 and 6a of Appendix G). The put/call fabricated short sale will almost always be superior to shorting stock since the purchased put will usually be cheaper than the call sold (a net credit to your account) and there are no dividends to pay out on shorted stock. Also, fabricated short sales are not confronted by the uptick rule, and are not subject to short squeezes or involuntary buy-ins.

Table 5-7 illustrates the versatility of listed options. For each 10 Zenith Radio bonds held long, 2 in-the-money August 20 puts are purchased and 4 out-of-the-money August 20 calls are sold. The hedge position, therefore, involves the fabricated short sale of 200 shares of stock plus two extra call options. As shown by the

TABLE 5-6

Risk-reward analysis for Zenith Radio convertible bond combined with put options, April 1981

Hedge workout for bullish posture

Position:

Buy 10 bonds at 100   = $10,000
Buy 2 August 20 puts at 3   = +   600
Investment   = $10,600

Risk-reward analysis:

Prices at expiration					
Stock	9	15	18	20	27
Bond	77	91	100	107	135
Put	11	5	2	0	0
Profit or (loss)					
Bonds	(2300)	(900)	700	700	3500
Puts	1600	400	(200)	(600)	(600)
Bond interest for four months ..	280	280	280	280	280
Net profit or (loss)	(420)	(220)	80	380	3180
Percent return					
Four months	− 4.0	− 2.1	+ 0.8	+ 3.6	+ 30.0
Annualized	− 11.9	− 6.3	+ 2.4	+ 10.8	+ 90.0

EXHIBIT 5-5
Profit profile for convertible/put option hedge position
in Zenith Radio (from Table 5-6)

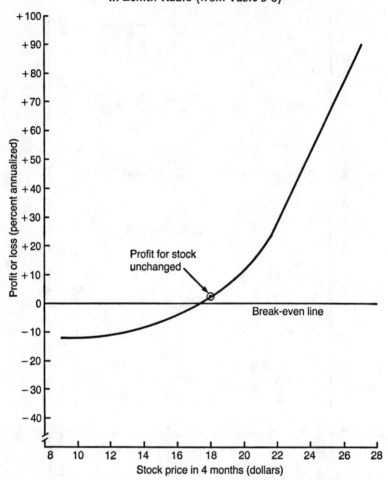

TABLE 5-7

Risk-reward analysis for Zenith Radio convertible bond combined with put and call options, April 1981

Hedge workout for neutral posture

Position:

Buy 10 bonds at 100	=	$10,000
Buy 2 August 20 puts at 3	= +	600
Sell 4 August 20 calls at 1½	= −	600
Investment	=	$10,000

Risk-reward analysis:

Prices at expiration					
Stock · · · · · · · · · · · · ·	9	15	18	20	27
Bond · · · · · · · · · · · · ·	77	91	100	107	135
Put · · · · · · · · · · · · ·	11	5	2	0	0
Call · · · · · · · · · · · · ·	0	0	0	0	7
Profit or (loss)					
Bonds · · · · · · · · · ·	(2300)	(900)	0	700	3500
Puts · · · · · · · · · ·	1600	400	(200)	(600)	(600)
Calls · · · · · · · · · ·	600	600	600	600	(2200)
Bond interest for four months · · ·	280	280	280	280	280
Net profit or (loss) · · · · ·	180	380	680	980	980
Percent return					
Four months · · · · ·	+ 1.8	+ 3.8	+ 6.8	+ 9.8	+ 9.8
Annualized · · · · · ·	+ 5.4	+ 11.4	+ 20.4	+ 29.4	+ 29.4

risk-reward analysis of Table 5-7 and the profit profile of Exhibit 5-6, the net results provide an attractive alternative to money market instruments.

Managing a convertible/option hedge portfolio

The portfolio management guidelines for convertible/stock hedges of Chapter 4 (research, risk-reward analysis, hedge selection, and order execution) are all vitally important to the success of any program involving listed put and call options. The major difference between the two strategies lies in the area of portfolio monitoring. Convertible/stock hedging is a relatively straightforward strategy to monitor, whereas the use of puts and calls involves a greater number of variables that must be considered. Here are suggested management tactics for hedgers desiring a low-risk bullish posture in the market.

1. Put options should be purchased if premium levels are below normal, while call options should be sold when premiums are above normal. If premium levels are about average—and they are most of the time—then the choice depends on one's individual preference. I generally favor the sale of calls because this approach provides greater profits under most market conditions. The convertible/put option hedge will produce higher profits during strong market advances, but I'm willing to forego occasional large profits for more consistent returns from year to year.

2. The convertible security should be held only as long as it offers a favorable market advantage over its underlying common stock. When it loses its advantage, the entire position should be closed out even though the option may have some time remaining to its expiration date (the exception would be to hold the convertible for a short while longer to attain long-term capital gains for those investors in high tax brackets.)

3. When out-of-the-money puts or calls decline to very low prices (e.g., $\frac{1}{8}$ or $\frac{1}{4}$), they no longer provide the protection they did when the hedge was established. They should be closed out and replaced with other option's offering better protection if

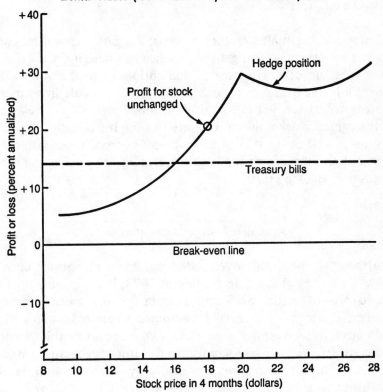

EXHIBIT 5-6
Profit profile for convertible/put-call option hedge in
Zenith Radio (from Table 5-7) versus Treasury bills

there are any available. If not, the convertible should be reevaluated and a conscious decision made to hold it unhedged or to sell it.

These are the major factors to consider, but you will be confronted by others as you gain experience in managing a portfolio using puts and calls. The use of listed options in combination with convertible securities is probably the most difficult investment strategy to master, yet is probably the most rewarding. In relation to the capital market line of Exhibit 1 of the Introduction, its risk posture is well below that of the balanced approach, but it has the potential to outperform the high-risk strategy of buying common stocks over the long term.

Actual investment experience

Although I have employed listed put and call options extensively since they first began trading in 1973, it is not possible for me to present actual performance data for any specific option strategy. Options were usually combined with convertibles that were attractive investments on their own merits. For this reason, the convertibles were frequently held without a related option position. Options were bought or sold only when premium levels and other factors were attractive. However, as I will show in the next chapter, accounts employing listed options (along with other convertible strategies) performed favorably, compared to conventional investment instruments.

APPENDIX G

Basic put and call option strategies

The exhibits presented in the following pages provide a risk-reward analysis and a profit profile for each of the following basic strategies and their alternates:

Bullish strategies

1. Buy 100 shares of stock.
1a. Buy one call and sell one put.
2. Buy 100 shares of stock and buy one put.
2a. Buy one call.
3. Buy 100 shares of stock and sell one call.
3a. Sell one put.

Bearish strategies

4. Short 100 shares of stock and sell one put.
4a. Sell one call.
5. Short 100 shares of stock and buy one call.
5a. Buy one put.
6. Short 100 shares of stock.
6a. Buy one put and sell one call.

Other strategies

7. Buy 100 shares of stock, buy one put, and sell one call.
7a. Buy T bills.

8. Buy 100 shares of stock and sell two calls.

8a. Sell one put and sell one call (straddle).

9. Short 100 shares of stock and buy two calls.

9a. Buy one put and buy one call (straddle).

Each of the basic strategies involves the purchase or short sale of common stock, while the alternates exclude the use of stock. Before investors select a particular strategy, or its alternate, they should prepare a risk-reward analysis similar to the examples shown in the following pages. The risk-reward calculations in the examples are based on these assumptions:

The common stock is trading at $20 and pays no dividend.

A six-month put option having an exercise price of $20 is trading at $2 ($200 for each put on 100 shares of stock).

A six-month call option having an exercise price of $20 is trading at $3 ($300 for each call on 100 shares of stock).

The investment for each position is $2,000. Unused funds or premiums received from the sale of options are invested in Treasury bills yielding 10 percent.

Brokerage commissions are excluded for ease of illustration; however, some strategies involve few commission dollars, while others are quite costly (depending on portfolio turnover, and so on). For example, when comparing strategy 1 with its alternate 1a, the long-term investor should buy the common stock instead of turning over put and call options every few months (lower commissions plus the tax advantages of long-term capital gains). Traders may find it more economical to use options.

Note that when a basic strategy involves the short sale of common stock (strategies 4, 5, 6, and 9), the alternates are far superior. This is because the short seller does not get the use of the short sale proceeds, while the difference in premiums between the put and call options reflects the current value of money (strategy 7) and is immediately available.

EXHIBIT G-1
Basic option strategies 1 and 1a

	Prices at expiration date		
Stock	10	20	30
Call	0	0	10
Put	10	0	0

Strategy 1: Buy 100 shares of stock
Profit or (loss) on stock . . . . (1000)   0   1000

Strategy 1a: Buy one call and sell one put
Profit or (loss) on call . . . . (300) (300) 700
Profit or (loss) on put . . . . (800) 200 200
Interest earned on $1,900 in T bills . . . . . . <u>95</u> <u>95</u> <u>95</u>
Total profit or (loss) . . . . (1005) (5) 995

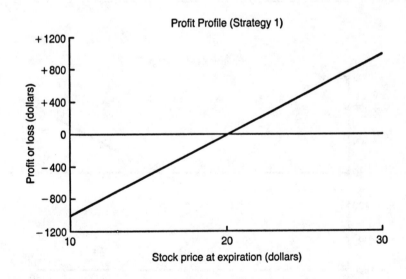

Profit Profile (Strategy 1)

EXHIBIT G-2
Basic option strategies 2 and 2a

		Prices at expiration date		
Stock		10	20	30
Call		0	0	10
Put		10	0	0

Strategy 2: Buy 100 shares of stock and
  buy one put

Profit or (loss) on stock		(1000)	0	1000
Profit or (loss) on put		800	(200)	(200)
Interest charge on $200		(10)	(10)	(10)
Total profit or (loss)		(210)	(210)	790

Strategy 2a: Buy one call

Profit or (loss) on call		(300)	(300)	700
Interest earned on $1,700 in T bills		85	85	85
Total profit or (loss)		(215)	(215)	785

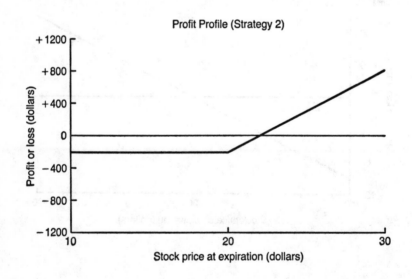

Profit Profile (Strategy 2)

EXHIBIT G-3
Basic option strategies 3 and 3a

	Prices at expiration date		
Stock	10	20	30
Call	0	0	10
Put	10	0	0

Strategy 3: Buy 100 shares of stock and
sell one call
Profit or (loss) on stock	(1000)	0	1000
Profit or (loss) on call	300	300	(700)
Interest earned on $300 in T bills	15	15	15
Total profit or (loss)	(685)	315	315

Strategy 3a: Sell one put
Profit or (loss) on put	(800)	200	200
Interest earned on $2,200 in T bills	110	110	110
Total profit or (loss)	(690)	310	310

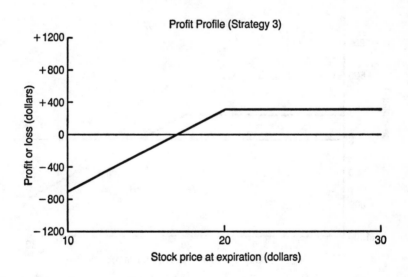

Profit Profile (Strategy 3)

EXHIBIT G-4
Basic option strategies 4 and 4a

	Prices at expiration date		
Stock	10	20	30
Call	0	0	10
Put	10	0	0

Strategy 4: Short 100 shares of stock and
  sell one put
Profit or (loss) on stock 1000   0   (1000)
Profit or (loss) on put .... (800)   200   200
Interest earned on $2,200 in T bills 110   110   110
Total profit or (loss) 310   310   (690)

Strategy 4a: Sell one call
Profit or (loss) on call 300   300   (700)
Interest earned on $2,300 in T bills 115   115   115
Total profit or (loss) 415   415   (585)

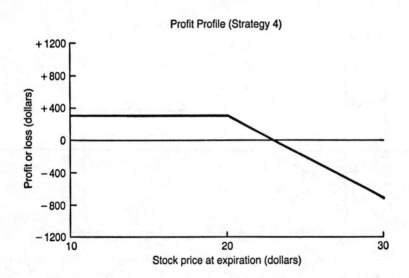

Profit Profile (Strategy 4)

EXHIBIT G-5
Basic option strategies 5 and 5a

	Prices at expiration date		
Stock	10	20	30
Call	0	0	10
Put	10	0	0

Strategy 5: Short 100 shares of stock and buy one call

Profit or (loss) on stock	1000	0	(1000)
Profit or (loss) on call	(300)	(300)	700
Interest earned on $1,700 in T bills	85	85	85
Total profit or (loss)	785	(215)	(215)

Strategy 5a: Buy one put

Profit or (loss) on put	800	(200)	(200)
Interest earned on $1,800 in T bills	90	90	90
Total profit or (loss)	890	(110)	(110)

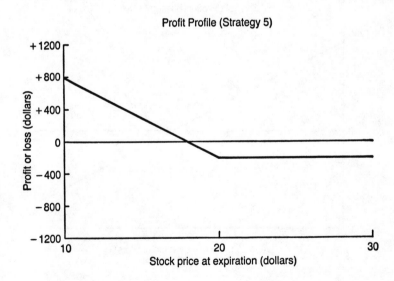

Profit Profile (Strategy 5)

EXHIBIT G-6
Basic option strategies 6 and 6a

	Prices at expiration date		
Stock	10	20	30
Call	0	0	10
Put	10	0	0

Strategy 6: Short 100 shares of stock
Profit or (loss) on stock	1000	0	(1000)
Interest earned on $2,000 in T bills	100	100	100
Total profit or (loss)	1100	100	(900)

Strategy 6a: Buy one put and sell one call
Profit or (loss) on put	800	(200)	(200)
Profit or (loss) on call	300	300	(700)
Interest earned on $2,100 in T bills	105	105	105
Total profit or (loss)	1205	205	(795)

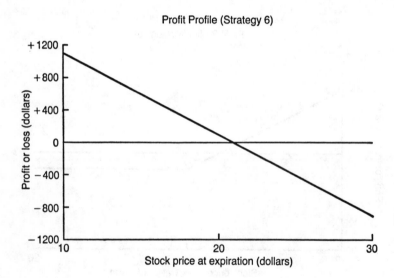

Profit Profile (Strategy 6)

EXHIBIT G-7
Basic option strategies 7 and 7a

	Prices at expiration date		
Stock	10	20	30
Call	0	0	10
Put	10	0	0

Strategy 7: Buy 100 shares of stock, buy one
put, and sell one call

Profit or (loss) on stock	(1000)	0	1000
Profit or (loss) on put	800	(200)	(200)
Profit or (loss) on call	300	300	(700)
Interest earned on $100 in T bills	5	5	5
Total profit or (loss)	105	105	105

Strategy 7a: Buy T bills

Interest earned on $2,000 in T bills	100	100	100

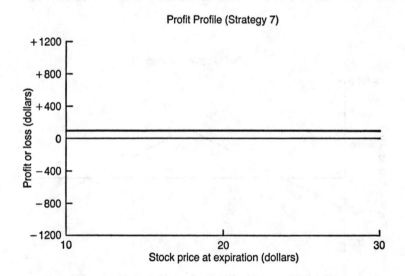

Profit Profile (Strategy 7)

EXHIBIT G-8
Basic option strategies 8 and 8a

	Prices at expiration date		
Stock ...	10	20	30
Call ...	0	0	10
Put ...	10	0	0

Strategy 8: Buy 100 shares of stock and
    sell two calls

Profit or (loss) on stock	(1000)	0	1000
Profit or (loss) on calls...............	600	600	(1400)
Interest earned on $600 in T bills	30	30	30
Total profit or (loss)	(370)	630	(370)

Strategy 8a: Sell one put and sell one call
    (straddle)

Profit or (loss) on put	(800)	200	200
Profit or (loss) on call	300	300	(700)
Interest earned on $2,500 in T bills	125	125	125
Total profit or (loss)	(375)	625	(375)

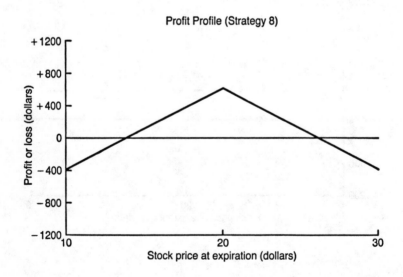

Profit Profile (Strategy 8)

EXHIBIT G-9
Basic option strategies 9 and 9a

		Prices at expiration date		
Stock	10	20	30
Call	0	0	10
Put	10	0	0

Strategy 9: Short 100 shares of stock and
  buy two calls

Profit or (loss) on stock	1000	0	(1000)
Profit or (loss) on calls.................	(600)	(600)	1400
Interest earned on $1,400 in T bills	70	70	70
Total profit or (loss)	470	(530)	470

Strategy 9a: Buy one put and buy one call
  (straddle)

Profit or (loss) on put	800	(200)	(200)
Profit or (loss) on call	(300)	(300)	700
Interest earned on $1,500 in T bills	75	75	75
Total profit or (loss)	575	(425)	575

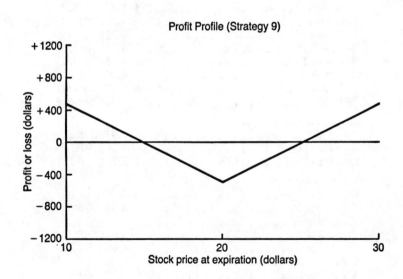

Profit Profile (Strategy 9)

APPENDIX H

Convertibles on stocks having listed options, August 1981

Industry group	Convertible description
Aerospace:	
Boeing	8.875 -06
General Dynamics	$ 4.25A pfd.
Lear Siegler Inc.	$ 2.25 pfd.
Lockheed	$11.25 pfd.
Lockheed	4.250 -92
McDonnell Douglas	4.750 -91
Rockwell Intl.	$ 4.75 pfd.
Rockwell Intl.	$ 1.35 pfd.
Rockwell Intl.	4.250 -91
TRW Inc.	$ 4.40 Series 1
TRW Inc.	$ 4.50 Series 3
Agricultural equipment:	
Allis-Chalmers	$ 5.875C pfd.
Deere & Co.	5.500 -01
Intl. Harvester	$ 5.76C pfd.
Air transport:	
Delta Air Lines	6.500 -86
Tiger Intl.	8.625 -05
Trans World	$ 2.00 pfd.
Trans World	$ 2.66C pfd.
Trans World	4.000 -92
Trans World	5.000 -94
Trans World	12.000 -05
UAL Inc.	5.000 -91
UAL Inc.	4.250 -92
U.S. Air	$ 3.00C pfd.
U.S. Air	8.250 -05

APPENDIX H *(continued)*

Industry group	Convertible description
Aluminum:	
Reynolds Metals	$ 4.50 pfd.
Reynolds Metals	4.500 -91
Auto/truck:	
Ford Motor	4.500 -96
Ford Motor	4.875 -98
Signal Cos.	5.500 -94
Bank:	
Chase Manhattan	4.875 -93
Chase Manhattan	6.500 -96
Citicorp	5.750 -00
Brewing:	
Anheuser-Busch	9.000 -05
Building:	
U.S. Home	5.500 -96
Walter, Jim	$ 1.60 pfd.
Walter, Jim	5.750 -91
Chemical:	
Allied Corp..	7.750 -05
GAF Corp.	$ 1.20 pfd.
Grace (W.R.)	4.250 -90
Grace (W.R.)	6.500 -96
Hercules	6.500 -99
Intl. Minerals & Chem..	4.000 -91
Minn. Mining & Mfg.	4.250 -97
Union Carbide	10.000 -06
Coal and uranium:	
Mapco	10.000 -05
Pittston	9.200 -04
Computer/data processing:	
Computer Sciences	6.000 -94
Control Data	3.750 -89
Data Point	8.875 -06
Mohawk Data Sciences	5.500 -94
Prime Computer	10.000 -00
Storage Technology	10.250 -00
Storage Technology	9.000 -01
Wang Labs.	9.500 -05
Distilling:	
Heublein	4.500 -97
Natl. Distillers & Chem.	4.500 -92

APPENDIX H *(continued)*

Industry group	Convertible description
Drug:	
Bristol-Myers	$ 2.00 pfd.
Pfizer	4.000 -97
Pfizer	8.7-0 00
Searle (G.D.)	5.250 -89
Searle (G.D.)	4.500 -92
Syntex	$ .75B pfd.
Electrical equipment:	
RCA Corp.	$ 4.00 pfd.
RCA Corp.	$ 2.125 pfd.
RCA Corp.	4.500 -92
Electric utilities:	
Commonwealth Edison	$ 1.425 pfd.
Consolidated Edison	$ 6.00 pfd.
Duke Power	$ 6.75 pfd.
Virginia Elec. & Power	3.625 -86
Electronics:	
General Instrument	4.250 -85
General Instrument	5.000 -92
Zenith Radio	8.375 -05
Finance:	
Household Intl.	$ 2.375 pfd.
Household Intl.	$ 2.50 pfd.
Food processing:	
Beatrice Foods	$ 3.38A pfd.
Norton Simon	$ 1.60A pfd.
Ralston Purina	5.750 -00
Health care/hospital supplies:	
Baxter Travenol Labs	4.375 -91
Baxter Travenol Labs	4.750 -01
Becton Dickinson	4.125 -88
Becton Dickinson	5.000 -89
Becton Dickinson	10.750 -06
Hotel/gaming:	
Hilton Hotels	5.500 -95
Holiday Inns	Series A
Holiday Inns	9.625 -05
MGM Grand Hotels	9.500 -00
Insurance:	
INA Corp.	$ 1.90C pfd.
MGIC Investment	5.000 -93
Traveler's	$ 2.00 pfd.

APPENDIX H *(continued)*

Industry group	Convertible description
Machinery:	
Caterpillar Tractor	5.500 -00
Medical services:	
Hospital Corp. Amer.	8.750 -06
National Medical Enter.	9.000 -06
Metals and mining:	
Amax Inc.	$ 3.00 pfd.
Newmont Mining	$ 4.50 pfd.
Texasgulf Inc.	$ 3.00 pfd.
Multiform:	
Avco	$ 3.20 pfd.
Avco	5.500 -93
City Investing	$ 2.00 pfd.
City Investing	7.500 -90
Fuqua Industries	$ 1.25B pfd.
Fuqua Industries	5.750 -88
Gulf & Western Inds.	$ 3.875C pfd.
Gulf & Western Inds.	$ 2.50D pfd.
Intl. Tel. & Tel.	$ 4.00H pfd.
Intl. Tel. & Tel.	$ 4.50I pfd.
Intl. Tel. & Tel.	$ 4.00J pfd.
Intl. Tel. & Tel.	$ 4.00K pfd.
Intl. Tel. & Tel.	$ 2.25N pfd.
Intl. Tel. & Tel.	$ 5.00O pfd.
Intl. Tel. & Tel.	8.625 -00
Litton Industries Inc.	3.500 -87
United Technologies	$ 3.875 pfd.
United Technologies	$ 2.55 pfd.
Whittaker	4.500 -88
Natural gas:	
El Paso	6.000 -93A
Office equipment and supply:	
Pitney-Bowes	$ 2.12 pfd.
Xerox Corporation	6.000 -95
Oilfield services:	
McDermott	$ 2.20 pfd.
Reading & Bates	$ 2.125 pfd.
Packaging and containers:	
Owens-Illinois	$ 4.75 pfd.
Owens-Illinois	4.500 -92
Paper and forest products:	
Champion Intl.	4.500 -84
Champion Intl.	$ 1.20 pfd.

APPENDIX H *(continued)*

Industry group	Convertible description
Paper and forest products *(continued)*	
Champion Intl.	$ 4.60 pfd.
Georgia Pacific	5.250 -96
Georgia Pacific	$ 2.24A pfd.
Georgia Pacific	$ 2.24B pfd.
Weyerhauser	$ 2.80 pfd.
Weyerhauser	$ 4.50A pfd.
Petroleum:	
Amerada Hess	$ 3.50 pfd.
Ashland Oil	$ 3.96 pfd.
Ashland Oil	4.750 -93
Atlantic Richfield	$ 3.00 pfd.
Atlantic Richfield	$ 2.80 pfd.
Charter Co. Depositary Preferred	
Coastal Corp.	$ 1.83 pfd.
Dorchester Gas	8.500 -05
Inexco Oil	8.500 -00
Natomas	$ 4.00C pfd.
Occidental Petroleum	$ 2.16 pfd.
Occidental Petroleum	$ 3.60 pfd.
Occidental Petroleum	$ 4.00 pfd.
Pennzoil	5.250 -96
Pogo Producing	8.000 -05
Sun Co.	$ 2.25 pfd.
Publishing	
Time	$ 1.575B pfd.
Time	$ 4.50C pfd.
Railroad resources:	
Santa Fe Inds.	6.250 -98
Union Pacific	4.750 -99
Recreation:	
Bally Mfg.	6.000 -98
Brunswick	$ 2.40 pfd.
Brunswick	10.000 -06
Retail store:	
K Mart	6.000 -99
Woolworth (F.W.)	$ 2.20A pfd.
Savings and loan:	
Federal Natl. Mtg.	4.375 -96
Securities brokerage:	
Dean Witter Reynolds	10.000 -05
E. F. Hutton Group	9.500 -05
Merrill Lynch	9.250 -05

APPENDIX H *(concluded)*

Industry group	Convertible description
Soft drink:	
Pepsico	4.750 -96
Steel:	
LTV Corp.	Spl. C1 AA
LTV Corp.	Part. Ser. 1
United States Steel	15.750 -01
Telecommunications:	
Amer. Tel. & Teleg.	$ 4.00 pfd.
Continental Tel.	5.250 -86
Gen. Tel. & Electrs.	$ 2.50 pfd.
Gen. Tel. & Electrs.	4.000 -90
Gen. Tel. & Electrs.	5.000 -92
Gen. Tel. & Electrs.	6.250 -96
Western Union	$ 4.60 pfd.
Western Union	$ 4.90 pfd.
Western Union	5.250 -97
Tobacco:	
Reynolds Inds.	$ 2.25 pfd.
Trucking/trans. leasing:	
Greyhound	6.500 -90
Greyhound	6.000 -86

Note: Certain convertibles are described by different names than the companies shown. For example, the Allied Corporation convertible bond was issued by Textron (against Allied stock held by Textron) and trades as Textron 7¾s of 2005.

CHAPTER 6

The convertible strategies line

This book presented a number of strategies which I believe are superior to traditional investments. A superior investment strategy can be defined as one that promises an above-average return for any given level of risk. In addition, the higher expected return should more than compensate for the extra time and expense required to manage the strategy, compared to more passive buy-and-hold tactics.

For any strategy to be termed *superior* it must, above all, *make good sense.* I have asked you to believe the *mathematically under-valued* convertible securities presented in this book are superior, based on an *objective* reasoning process you can verify for yourself. Most recommendations offered by the investment community, no matter how well "researched," are highly *subjective.* However, they are ruled by the same laws of probability as the rest of the investment world, and, while some succeed, others fail. Converti-bles provide a way to determine before buying what the chances of success will be. Through the use of convertibles you can avoid having to take someone's word that your investments will perform well. Common sense is what enables you to predict whether a particular strategy involving convertibles should succeed.

A superior strategy should also be *supported by actual invest-ment experience.* There are a few exceptions to this rule. It is not always practical to wait for a record to develop, since a strategy's advantage could disappear during the time experience is being gained. For example, when listed call options first began trading in 1973, it was obvious to professional hedgers that premiums were too high and that calls should be sold instead of purchased. By the time the investment community awakened to this fact, and brought mutual funds to the market in 1977, premium levels had declined precipitously. Thus, covered call writing (against common stock) became a losing strategy while the concept was being "proven" between 1973 and 1977.

In contrast, convertible strategies presented in this book *are supported by ongoing experience.* Undervalued convertibles were theoretically sound when I began investing seriously 15 years ago and they offer comparable advantages today. Specific strategies involving convertibles have changed over the years but the general concepts, based on mathematical measurements of under- and over-valuation, have not.

Exhibit 6-1 displays today's strategies positioned on the convertible strategies line. The capital market line (Exhibit 1 of the Introduction) is also shown for comparison. You will see that results expected at any level of risk are superior for the convertible strategies.

Each convertible strategy is depicted as falling neatly on the straight line only as a matter of convenience. The precise location of any undervalued convertible (or convertible hedge position) will be the result of numerous factors, including the degree of its undervaluation. For example, blue-chip convertibles with options available have a wider following among investors and are not as undervalued, on average, as aggressive convertibles of lesser-known companies. In spite of these variables, however, I believe the convertible strategies line is a useful tool when comparing alternatives and for defining investment objectives that can be measured by appropriate market indexes.

Strategies involving undervalued convertibles are available to meet anyone's desired risk posture. The following table summarizes and compares them to the traditional stock and bond combinations.

Convertible strategy	Risk posture compared to traditional portfolios	
	Percent stocks	Percent bonds
Aggressive convertibles	100	0
All undervalued convertibles	75	25
Low-risk convertibles	50	50
Convertible/option hedges	25	75
Convertible/stock hedges	0	100

EXHIBIT 6-1
Selected convertible strategies compared to the capital market line

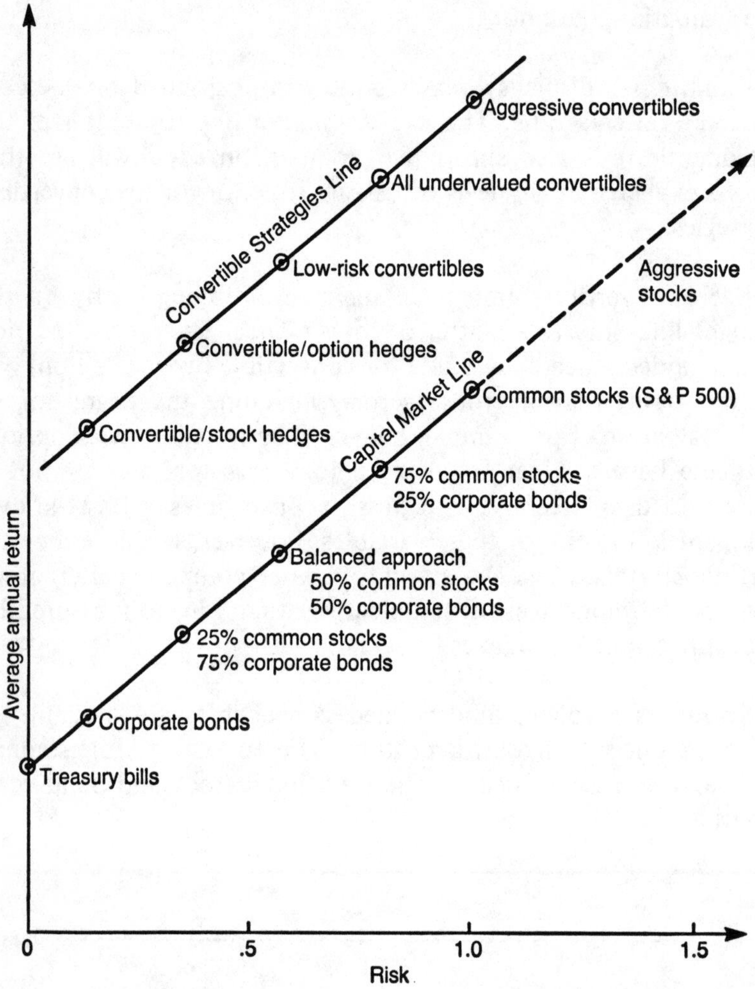

Designing your portfolio

The convertible strategy you select should depend on various factors, including your desired risk posture, federal income tax bracket, and portfolio management ability (if you plan to do it yourself). The most straightforward strategy, having a risk posture comparable to the balanced approach, uses low-risk convertibles. Here a conservative investor can choose convertibles of well-known companies with the help of readily available data from a number of different sources. Following the guidelines of Chapter 3, the portfolio can be managed without an extraordinary amount of time and effort.

Investors desiring a lower-risk posture, and skilled in evaluating listed options, may wish to confine their convertible selections to those having puts and calls on their underlying common stocks. When premium levels and other factors are favorable, puts and calls may be purchased or sold for protective purposes following the guidelines of Chapter 5, recognizing that options usually reduce potential opportunity for profit in exchange for risk reduction.

Very conservative investors (or investors in high income tax brackets) should employ convertible/stock hedges. These hedges are highly suitable for pension funds when purchased for cash. They offer individual investors the opportunity for substantial aftertax profits when purchased on margin because net profits should be mostly long-term capital gains.

The one strategy I have not employed by itself is aggressive convertibles. It involves dealing with lesser-known companies where good research is seldom available. Because of the constraints dictated by managing clients' assets, and personal risk-averse biases, I have chosen to use these higher-risk securities solely for hedging purposes. Remember that the inherent safety of the hedge obviates the need to know the company well or to depend heavily on a specific company's success.

For clients desiring a high degree of diversification, I usually employ a combination of the three low-risk strategies. The precise dollar relationships among these alternatives can be expected to change as market conditions change, but the risk posture should usually be close to that of a 25/75 stock/bond combination portfolio.

Actual investment experience

Table 6-1 and Exhibit 6-2 illustrate the risks and rewards of hedging; they compare the composite quarterly performance record for my largest managed convertible hedge accounts with appropriate market indexes for the six-year period ending December 31, 1981. As shown by Table 6-1, the annual compounded rate of return for hedging—16.8 percent—far surpassed all traditional investment instruments during that time.

The risk level of the composite convertible hedge portfolio was approximately that of a combination of 25 percent common stocks and 75 percent corporate bonds. Its 154 percent gain for the six-year period compared with 32 percent for the 25/75 combination.

The performance data of Table 6-1 also illustrate the importance of controlling risk for long-term success. While the hedge accounts underperformed common stocks during the bull market of 1979-80 (31 percent versus 57 percent for the S&P 500 and 35 percent for the Dow), their higher returns during the weaker stock market years resulted in greater overall performance. The 154 percent gain from hedging compares with 83 percent and 42 percent for the higher risk S&P 500 and the Dow Jones Industrials.

A final word from the author

Any investor, whether managing personal assets or acting as a trustee of a pension fund, has a responsibility to make informed investment decisions. My hope is that this book has helped to convince you that convertible strategies offer some of the best ways to secure a favorable outcome. The opportunities available in undervalued convertibles are as plentiful as ever. This expanding

TABLE 6-1
Composite record for largest managed convertible hedge accounts versus market indexes (total returns)

Year and quarter	Hedge accounts*	T bills	Bonds†	Stocks‡	Stocks§
1976 -1 . . . . . . +	2.4%	+ 1.2%	+ 4.2%	+18.3%	+15.0%
-2 . . . . . . +	4.5	+ 1.3	+ 0.3	+ 1.3	+ 2.4
-3 . . . . . . +	8.7	+ 1.3	+ 5.6	− 0.3	+ 1.9
-4 . . . . . . +	9.4	+ 1.2	+ 7.5	+ 2.5	+ 3.1
1977 -1 . . . . . . +	6.1	+ 1.1	− 2.3	− 7.5	− 7.5
-2 . . . . . . +	3.3	+ 1.2	+ 3.9	+ 0.9	+ 3.2
-3 . . . . . . +	7.2	+ 1.3	+ 1.1	− 6.3	− 2.8
-4 . . . . . . +	2.7	+ 1.5	− 0.8	− 0.5	− 0.3
1978 -1 . . . . . . +	5.2	+ 1.6	0.0	− 7.5	− 4.9
-2 . . . . . . +	4.7	+ 1.6	− 1.1	+ 9.6	+ 8.5
-3 . . . . . . +	8.4	+ 1.8	+ 3.1	+ 7.1	+ 8.7
-4 . . . . . . −	1.9	+ 2.0	− 2.0	− 5.6	− 5.0
1979 -1 . . . . . . +	5.2	+ 2.3	+ 1.6	+ 8.6	+ 7.1
-2 . . . . . . +	8.8	+ 2.3	+ 4.5	− 0.9	+ 2.7
-3 . . . . . . +	3.5	+ 2.3	− 2.0	+ 5.8	+ 7.6
-4 . . . . . . −	2.9	+ 2.8	− 7.9	− 3.0	+ 0.1
1980 -1 . . . . . . −	8.8	+ 3.1	−13.5	− 4.8	− 4.1
-2 . . . . . . +	16.3	+ 2.7	+25.1	+12.1	+13.5
-3 . . . . . . +	6.0	+ 2.1	−11.1	+ 8.9	+11.2
-4 . . . . . . +	1.1	+ 3.1	+ 1.2	+ 4.8	+ 9.5
1981 -1 . . . . . . +	8.4	+ 3.4	− 1.1	+ 5.6	+ 1.4
-2 . . . . . . +	2.6	+ 3.5	− 2.2	− 1.3	− 2.3
-3 . . . . . . −	8.0	+ 3.7	− 9.3	−11.6	−10.3
-4 . . . . . . +	5.4	+ 3.0	+12.9	+ 4.6	+ 6.9
Cumulative returns for six years	+153.6%	+66.3%	+11.4%	+41.6%	+82.6%
Annual compounded rate of return . . . . . +	16.8%	+ 8.8%	+ 1.8%	+ 6.0%	+10.6%

*Based on the largest account under management each quarter. Returns include expenses for order execution and account management.

†Based on the Salomon Brothers High-Grade Long-Term Corporate Bond Index. Returns exclude order execution and account management expenses.

‡Based on the Dow Jones Industrial Average. Returns exclude order execution and account management expenses.

§Based on the Standard & Poor's 500 Stock Index. Returns exclude order execution and account management expenses.

EXHIBIT 6-2
Composite record for largest managed convertible hedge
accounts versus market indexes (Table 6-1)

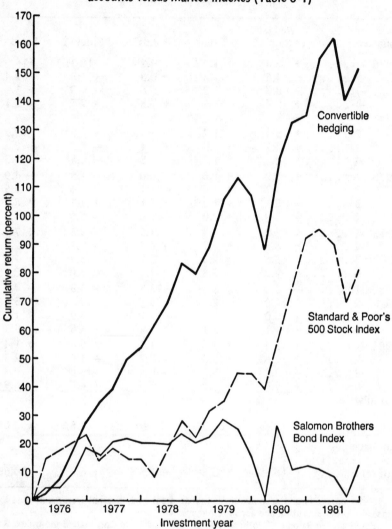

sector of our capital markets remains inefficient and I see no significant trends to the contrary.

In my previous books I assumed that, armed with knowledge gained from the books and following the guidelines I had set forth, readers could enter the investment arena themselves and do battle, with the outcome assured. Now I am not so sure.

The areas of convertibles and convertible hedging strategies have become highly professionalized. Regardless of the sophisticated investment aids that individuals may have at their disposal (e.g., investment advisory services and personal computers), I have become convinced the keys to successful investing in these specialty areas are market experience and access to the ideas of other professionals.

Therefore, if you plan to employ the concepts presented in this book, I suggest using an experienced investment adviser to execute your chosen strategy. Should you decide to manage your own portfolio, work with a specialty stockbroker skilled in the selected area. Convertible strategies demand the best available talents.

GLOSSARY

Accrued interest.   Interest earned on a bond since its last interest payment date. The buyer of the bond pays the market price plus accrued interest to the seller and is entitled to the next interest payment in full. Exceptions include bonds in default and income bonds, which are traded flat (without accrued interest).

Adjustment of conversion terms.   Changes in conversion terms which may be provided for under the terms of the conversion privilege or by virtue of the implementation of an antidilution clause.

Antidilution clause.   Provisions contained in most convertibles which call for the adjustment of the conversion terms in the event of stock splits, stock dividends, or the sale of new stock at a price below the conversion price of existing convertibles. In some cases, no adjustment is made for small stock dividends (e.g. under five percent in any single year or ten percent during the life of the convertible).

Arbitrage.   A simultaneous purchase and sale of similar securities for an immediate profit upon conversion. This technique generally involves the purchase of a convertible bond or preferred that is trading at a price below its conversion value and the sale of its common stock.

Beta.   A tool for indentifying market risk by measuring the historical sensitivity of a stock's price movements to overall market fluctuations.

Bond indenture.   The contract under which bonds are issued. It describes such terms of the agreement as interest rate, interest payment dates, date of maturity, redemption terms, conversion privileges, and the security for the loan.

Bond price quotation.   Bonds are quoted as a percentage of par. Thus, *90* means 90 percent of a $1,000 bond, or $900. *110* means 110 percent of par or $1,100.

Break-even time.   The time period in which a convertible bond or preferred will recapture the premium paid over conversion value through extra income when bond interest or preferred dividends exceed the common stock's dividend.

Call price.   The amount of money a corporation is obliged to pay if it chooses to redeem its senior securities. In the case of bonds, the call price is usually expressed as a percentage of par. In the case of preferred stock, the call is the price per share. The call price normally starts somewhat above par and is reduced periodically.

Callable.   Term applying to securities which contain a provision giving the issuer the right to retire the issue prior to its maturity date.

Capital Market Line.   A graphical presentation of risk-reward relationships for various investment strategies.

Conversion parity.   The price at which the convertible must sell for it to equal the current market value of the common shares to be received upon conversion. If the convertible is trading at a premium above conversion parity, it is generally better to sell the convertible rather than to convert.

Conversion premium.   The difference between a convertible's market price and its conversion value expressed as a percentage above conversion value.

Conversion price.   The price at which the underlying common stock must trade at in order for the bond to be worth par value if converted.

Conversion value.   The worth of a convertible bond or preferred if it were converted into common stock. It equals the number of shares to be received upon conversion multiplied by the current market price of the common.

Convertible bond.   A bond which may be exchanged, at the option of the holder, into common stock or other securities in accordance with the terms of the bond indenture.

Convertible hedge.   A market strategy in which the investor buys or holds a convertible bond or preferred and sells call options or common stock short against it.

Convertible preferred stock.   An equity security, senior to the common stock, which may be exchanged, at the option of the holder, into common stock or other securities.

Convertible price curve.   A curve showing the expected convertible price for any stock price over the near-term future.

Convertible Strategies Line.   A graphical presentation of risk-reward relationships for various investment strategies involving undervalued convertibles.

Cumulative preferred.   A preferred stock which provides for omitted dividends (arrearages) to be paid before dividends may be paid on the company's common stock.

Current yield.   The interest or dividends paid annually by a company on a security, expressed as a percentage of the current market price of the security.

Default.   Failure of the bond issuer to meet a contract obligation, such as payment of interest, maintenance of working capital requirements, or payment of principal via a sinking fund or at maturity.

Delayed convertible.   A convertible security which does not become convertible until some future date.

Discounted bond.   A bond selling below par value.

Ex-dividend.   A preferred or common stock trading without its current dividend. The seller of the security on the ex-dividend date will receive the dividend.

Expiration of conversion privileges.   The date when a convertible's conversion privilege terminates.

Fabricated convertible.   The combination of warrants plus bonds which are usable for exercise purposes at par value in lieu of cash is called a fabricated convertible and is comparable to a regular convertible bond.

Forced conversion.   When convertibles are called for redemption, or there is an adverse change in their conversion terms, or an upcoming expiration date, the holders of convertibles may be forced to convert in order to capture conversion value.

Indirect convertible.   A convertible that is exchangeable into common stock via another convertible security.

Investment value.   The estimated value of a convertible bond or preferred stock without giving any consideration to its conversion privilege. Also known as the investment floor.

Investment value premium.   The difference between a convertible's market price and its investment value expressed as a percentage above investment value.

Market advantage.   A mathematical calculation to determine if a convertible offers risk-reward characteristics superior to a combination of common stock and straight bonds having the same risk as the convertible.

Maturity date.   A fixed date when the company must redeem a bond by paying the full face value to the bondholder.

Plus-cash convertible.   A convertible bond or convertible preferred stock which requires an additional cash payment upon conversion.

Premium over conversion value.   *See* "Conversion premium."

Premium over investment value.   *See* "Investment value premium."

Profit profile.   A graphical presentation of a risk-reward analysis to permit a visual comparison of investment alternatives.

Redemption.   The act of retiring part or all of a bond issue prior to its maturity date. When a convertible bond issue is called by the issuing company and the bond is selling above the redemption price, it is equivalent to a forced conversion of the issue.

Registered bond.   A bond which is issued in the name of the holder as opposed to a bearer bond which is issued with coupons attached. Interest is paid by check to the holder. Most convertible bonds are registered.

Risk-reward analysis.   A mathematical evaluation of a convertible (or convertible hedge) relative to its underlying common stock, used to identify superior investment alternatives.

Sinking fund provisions.   A requirement that the company begin retiring a convertible issue prior to its maturity date.

Stock equivalency.   A mathematical calculation to determine the precise combination of common stock and straight bonds having the same risk as the convertible.

Subordinated debenture.   A bond which is subject to the prior claim of other senior securities and usually not secured by any specific property. Most convertible bonds are subordinate to regular bonds issued by the company.

Synthetic convertible.   The combination of money market instruments and call options having risk-reward characteristics similar to convertible securities.

Undervalued convertible.   A convertible having a market advantage above 1.0.

Unit convertible.   A convertible which is exchangeable into a package of one or more securities which includes at least one security other than common stock.

Yield advantage.   The difference between the yield of a convertible and its underlying common stock.

Yield to maturity.   The effective yield of a bond, taking into account its premium or discount from par, if one were to hold it to maturity when it is expected to be redeemed by the company at par value.

INDEX

233